FARM TRACTOR
MILESTONES

R A N D Y   L E F F I N G W E L L

MBI Publishing Company

Dedication

*This book is dedicated to the wives, girlfriends, mothers, daughter, and sisters
of tractor enthusiasts throughout the world.
Without your endless support, love, and participation,
fewer of us would be able to enjoy
collecting, preserving, and showing these machines.*

First published in 2000 by MBI Publishing Company, 729 Prospect Avenue,
PO Box 1, Osceola, WI 54020-0001USA

Library of Congress Cataloging-in-Publication Data
Leffingwell, Randy
    Farm tractor milestones / Randy Leffingwell.
      p.cm.
    ISBN 0-7603-0730-X (hc.: alk. paper)
      1. Farm tractors—Design and construction—History. I. Title.
  TL 233.6.F37 L4423 2000
  631.3'72'0973—dc21   00-058390

On the front cover: Two radical departures: the Minneapolis-Moline Comfortractor
and the John Deere 4010. The Minne-Mo represented a belief that the tractor could
double as transportation. Sales were slow and the model was considered a failure. The
JD 4010 was one of the New Generation tractors Deere & Co. introduced to replace
the two-cylinder-powered tractors. The 4010 helped JD vault ahead of International
to become the number one tractor manufacturer by the mid-1960s.

On the frontispiece: A Farmall A resting at peace. The original Farmall's innovation
was its ability to cultivate, and the Model A's claim to fame was a nearly
unobstructed view of the ground during cultivation that IH dubbed "Culti-vision."

On the title page: The funky bathtub-shaped Wallis Cub pioneered the unit frame,
which was nothing more than a solid tub of steel encasing the engine and drivetrain.

On the back cover: Three of the most significant machines of early agriculture grace
the back cover: a John Deere Model D, a Farmall Regular, and an Oliver Hart-Parr
Row Crop 70.

Edited by Lee Klancher
Layout by Dan Perry and LeAnn Kuhlmann
Designed by Tom Heffron
Photo edit by Amy Glaser and Sara Perfetti

Printed in Hong Kong

Contents

Acknowledgments

I am most grateful to Dave Rogers at Case Historical Foundation, Racine, Wisconsin, for his great help in arranging for me to photograph the 1924 International Farmall QC 503.

Thanks also to Carroll "Kelly" Birkey, Paxton, Ilinois, for his recollections of International Harvester's 2+2 tractors.

I am greatly indebted to Frank Howard, Service Manager at Allied Systems, Sherwood, Oregon, for his stories and information about Wagner's agricultural tractors from the 1950s through the last one in 1975.

I owe deep gratitude to a number of individuals who opened collections to me in order to pull out a single tractor or two in order to produce this book. My deep thanks go to Dean & Marla Alling, Saugus, Clifornia; Allen and Cheryl Anderson, Arlington, Oregon; Mike, Linda, and Eric Androvich, Bowling Green, Ohio; Herc and Betty Bouris, Minnifee Valley, California; Dick and Shirley Carroll, Alta Vista, Kansas; Larry and Anita Clark, and Clifford and Carol Clark, Yakima, Washington; Dan and Janice Crist, and D. A. and Carole Crist, Quinter, Kansas; Laurence Darrach, Nicolaus, California; David and Kay Fulkerson, Manville, Illinois; Joe and Nancy Gnoss, Woodland, California; Jerry and Carmen Green, Madras, Oregon; Jack and Barbara Gustafson, Byron, Illinois; Ronald Gustafson, Penfield, Illinois; Jim and Sue Haley, Odell, Illinois; Darius, Lois, and Toni Harms, St. Joseph, Illinois; John Harvey, Wilmington, Delaware; Ellen Hector and the late Robert Hector, LaGrande, Oregon; Edith Heidrick and the late Joseph Heidrick Collection, and Joe and Susie Heidrick, Jr., Woodland, California; Keith Hinchley, Cambridge, Wisconsin; Bob and Jeanette Hinds, Rio Linda, California; Dave Jansen, Racine, Wisconsin; Travis, Shirley, and Wes Jorde, Rochester, Minnesota; Wendell and Mary Kelch, Bethel, Ohio; Bruce and Judy Keller, Kaukauna, Wisconsin; Walter and Lois Keller, Forrest Junction, Wisconsin; Lorie and Ray Kiefer, Mansfield, Ohio; Don Kleven, Kansasville, Wisconsin; Lester Layher, Wood River, and Kenny and Harland Layher, Grand Island, Nebraska; Tom Lean, Edgerton, Wisconsin; Wendell and Carolyn Lundberg, Richvale, California; Norm and Donna Meinert, Davis, Illinois; Roger and Marie, Gaylen, Eugene, and Martin Mohr, Denison, Iowa; Billy Montgomery, Columbia, Missouri; Dale Onsrud, Janesville, Wisconsin; Bill, Kim, and Will Peterson, and Bill and Barbara Peterson, Lowell, Indiana; Bob and Mary Pollock, Denison, Iowa; J. C. and Karen Rietmier, St. Joseph, Illinois; Bob and Gratia Sheppard, Goodyear, Arizona; Kevin and Patricia Timothy, Woodland, California; Carsten Van Borstel, Grass Valley, Oregon; and T. J. Waits, Bethel, Ohio.

I owe special thanks to all the individuals and families who allowed their tractors to be pictured in this book. They are: Herc and Betty Bouris, Sun City, CA, 1913 Case 40 Steam Traction Engine; Bill and Kim Peterson, Bill and Barbara Peterson, Sr.,Lowell, IN, 904 Hart-Parr 22-40 #1341; Dan and Janice Crist, D. A. and Carole Crist, Quinter, KS, 1911 Rumely E; Travis, Shirley, and Wes Jorde, Rochester, MN, 1914 Waterloo Boy Model R #1560; Laurence Darrach, Nicolaus, CA, 1917 Best 75; Dick and Shirley Carroll, Alta Vista, KS, 1914 Wallis Cub; Edith Heidrick, Woodland, CA, 1918 Fordson; Mike, Linda, and Eric Androvich, Bowling Green, OH, 1921 International 15-30 Gear Drive w/PTO; Lester Layher, Wood River, NE, Harland and Kenny Layher, Grand Island, NE, 1923 John Deere Model D; Wendell and Mary Kelch, Bethel, OH, Sheppard SD-1 1-cyl diesel air-cooled garden tractor; Tom Lean, Edgerton, WI, Red E Motor Cultivator; Dale Onsrud, Janesville, WI, 1956 Pennsylvania Panzer w/Briggs & Stratton, 1966 Minneapolis-Moline 110 w/Kohler; Wilbur and Janice Reil, Davis, CA, 1952 Pull-Away garden crawler; Case Historical, Dave Rogers, Manager, Photography and Communication Services, CASE Corporation, Racine, WI, 53404 USA, 1924 Farmall QC-503; Bob and Jeanne Hinds, Rio Linda, CA, 1937 Case CC Row Crop; Herc and Betty Bouris, Sun City, CA, 1936 Massey Harris GP 4 wheel drive; Allen and Cheryl Anderson, Arlington, OR, 1931 Caterpillar diesel 60 1C12; Norm and Donna Meinert, Davis, IL, 1935 Allis-Chalmers Model U on rubber; Keith Hinchley, Cambridge, WI, 1937 Oliver Row Crop 70 on tandem tiptoes; Bruce and Judy Keller, Brillion, WI, Walter and Lois Keller, Forest Junction, WI, 1937 Minneapolis-Moline Model U-DLX; Jack and Barbara Gustafson, Byron, IL, 1937 Allis-Chalmers Model B Waukesha; Joe and Nancy Gnoss, Woodland, CA, 1939 Ford 9N; Ellen Hector and the late Robert Hector, LaGrande, OR, 1946 Farmall Model A; Billy Montgomery, Columbia, MO, 1941 Minneapolis-Moline UTS-LPG; Lorrie and Ray Kiefer, Mansfield, OH, 1948 Allis-Chalmers Model G; Keith Hinchley, Cambridge, WI, 1948 Oliver 88 Diesel (wide front); Wendell and Mary Kelch, Bethel, OH, 1949 John Deere Model R Diesel; Roger and Marie Mohr, Gaylen, Eugene, and Martin Mohr, Denison, IA, Uni-Balor; Don Kleven, Kansasville, WI, 53139, 1954 International Harvester Super MTA highcrop; Bruce and Judy Keller, Brillion, WI, Walter and Lois Keller, Forest Junction, WI, 1962 Minneapolis Moline G-504 MFWD; Bob and Gratia Sheppard, Goodyear, AZ, 1956 Sheppard Diesel with Torque Converter transmission; Jerry and Carmen Green, Madras, OR, 1959 801 Select-O-Speed diesel on dual rears; Wendell and Mary Kelch, Bethel, OH, 1959 Ford 811 Logger Select-O-Speed; Larry and Anita Clark, Clifford and Carol Clark, Yakima, WA, 1965 Wagner WA17; Bruce and Judy Keller, Brillion, WI, Walter and Lois Keller, Forest Junction, WI, 1960 John

Deere 4010 high clearance LPG, 1960 John Deere 3010 Utility LPG; David T and Kay Fulkerson, Fulkerson Farms, Manville, IL, 1961 Allis-Chalmers D-19 diesel Turbo; Lester Layher, Wood River, NE, Harland and Kenny Layher, Grand Island, NE, 1964 John Deere 4020 with ROPS; Ronald Gustafson, Paxton, IL, 1967 International 656 Hydro #1531; J. C. and Karen Rietmier, St. Joseph, IL, 1978 International 3588 2+2; Kevin and Patricia Timothy, Woodland, CA, 1988 Caterpillar Challenger 65.

The concept of a "milestone" and the criteria for what make a tractor into a "milestone" grew out of several conversations with two very hard-working historians, Lorry Dunning, Davis, California, and Guy Fay, Madison, Wisconsin. I am very grateful to each of them for their help in creating this list and finding examples of each machine. I am further indebted to Guy Fay for his thoughts and research on the significance of each of these tractors then and now.

To all of you, and especially to each of the wives, girlfriends, mothers, and grandmothers, I offer my great thanks. I hope you enjoy your book.

—Randy Leffingwell

Introduction

Throughout the past ten years, a number of careful authors have produced very fine histories of mechanized farming in North America and Europe. Several of these writers have been engineers who made some of the history they reported. Many of these new books have dug into the nooks and crannies, archives and records, and they bring out sometimes-amazing details and stories of the challenges involved in producing reliable, saleable machines. It is many of those books that inspired this one.

The idea of *Farm Tractor Milestones* was born in 1996 when Lorry Dunning and I took a road trip together. Dunning, a consummate and careful historian with a deep knowledge of California farming and a thorough understanding of its impact on crops, practices, and techniques throughout the rest of the world, began trading with me observations on how those three issues differ from one region to the next. I wondered out loud if a book might be done tracing the history of farm tractor development based on introduction of new crops to farming. John Deere had made a Model P tractor specifically for potato farmers in Maine and New York. A number of manufacturers produced high clearance models in different configurations for cotton and sugar cane in the southeast and bedded vegetable farming in California. The scope of the book quickly grew to encyclopedic proportions and the joke between us became, "In volume seventeen we could deal with . . ."

Wrestling that concept back into manageable terms became the premise and challenge of *Farm Tractor Milestones*. Together with another trusted historian and friend, Guy Fay, we three developed a list of tractors that, in each case, significantly advanced the benchmark in mechanized farming. Our first list would have encompassed three volumes, a still unrealistic approach. One alone would have been devoted just to steam since nearly every improvement that ever appeared in internal combustion engines first showed up in steam (except, perhaps, for cultivating tractors.)

The final selection took nearly a year to whittle down to the 36 included in this book. By this time, our debates included Lee Klancher, who is editor to the three of us. Conversations frequently became passionate as one development weighed against another, one manufacturer's contributions against the others. What you will see and read here is the result: A history of the farm tractor demonstrating that each improvement grew out of previous developments, that the social, political and economic changes going on in the world had an impact, and that competition between manufacturers has greatly benefitted farmers and farming.

—Randy Leffingwell

Chapter 1

J. I. Case Threshing Machine Company's Steam Traction Engine

Internal combustion was the coming thing and Jesse Walrath was fascinated. He was the engine factory superintendent for J. I. Case Threshing Machine Company and responsible for product engineering. He had earned several patents for gas engines himself, the earliest in 1892, and he preached the subject to Case's receptive board of directors. On April 10, 1894, the board met William Paterson, a Scotsman from Stockton, California, who owned production rights for an unorthodox single-cylinder gas engine. Walrath pitched it and the board agreed to fund Paterson's project.

Outside North America's boardrooms, farmers were in an economic depression. Wheat prices had bottomed out at a quarter of what they were right after the Civil War, falling from $2.06 a bushel in 1866 to just 49 cents in 1894. While costs of everything were down, farmers' long-term acquisitions—farmland or machines bought in better times—ate up more of their reduced income. Case recognized that only improved technology could attract these tightened resources. Technology intrigued the average American.

Paterson built his engine at Case and installed it in a modified steam traction engine frame. The engine had a single cylinder in which two pistons operated toward each other. The combustion chamber was between the two pistons. Exhaust and inlet valves opened into the middle side of the cylinder. Electric ignition sparked through a cap screw set in the center of one piston, charged by a flat spring electrode in the cylinder wall. As the pistons came together, one passed the spring, making and breaking electrical contact, and making the spark. Timing was inexact and generally too late to derive maximum power or fuel efficiency. Walrath's young assistant, David

J. I. Case was very serious about its gasoline engine experiments. It hired William Paterson and later James Raymond to produce workable models the company could sell. When these failed, it fell back on George Morris and his European and English experience. Morris made side-crank engines work for Case.

9

produce many more engines than that. He contracted broilers and numerous castings to outside suppliers. Some of these firms had quality problems of their own, which made Case's problems worse.

During the 1860s and 1870s, American makers placed engines on the sides of the boilers. They suffered wear and reliability problems with long crankshafts that straddled the hot tanks. Engineers set the engines on top, believing this also improved balance, but Case's engines had design problems. They sold poorly overseas against such fine English makers as Ransome, Clayton and Shuttleworth, Marshall, or Fowler.

On January 26, 1895, the board met to consider two related subjects. Walrath appeared with Paterson. The board told Paterson he had to deliver a complete traction engine, workable to the satisfaction of Walrath and the board, by July 31, 1895. If he failed, Case would terminate his contract.

The board's second matter was to meet George Morris. Morris had worked at Ransome in England. He moved to Brantford, Ontario, opened his own firm, and designed a traction engine based on what he'd learned in England. This engine not only threshed, but it could pull plows. Morris later joined Case in England, traveling Europe trouble-shooting steam traction engines and studying the competition. He knew Case's shortcomings. Whether the board meant for Morris' presence that day to pressure Paterson is uncertain, but when they directed Morris to produce 16 of his steam traction engines, with 1 destined specifically to go to South America to sample the market there, it got the Scotsman's attention. Morris was to manage this production himself, answering to Walrath.

Paterson failed to deliver a working traction engine. The board discharged him on August 12. Soon after that, Walrath brought in James Raymond, who offered patents and designs on an entire line of stationary gas engines. Case, still willing to try gas engines, agreed to fund another attempt. The board saw the future, but the future just wasn't ready.

Raymond's engine proved to be difficult to manufacture. Worse, he misrepresented which patents he owned. Case found itself embroiled in a legal mess that matched its quality-control disasters. Looking for the source of its problems, the board saw Jesse Walrath and demanded "radical actions regarding shop practice and inspection of work." A spurt in orders for Case's engines in 1896, some 346, made things worse when Walrath's shops and suppliers couldn't deliver quickly enough to avoid losing orders. Walrath resigned on January 16, 1897.

Morris had worked quickly and successfully. He completed his first engine, number 6184, in June 1895. He finished more in the fall and winter and through 1896, he built both portable and traction

J. I. Case Threshing Machine Company adopted the eagle logo in 1894. The company named the eagle "Old Abe" and perched him atop the globe where he remained for 75 years, until 1969 when Tenneco Inc. assumed 91 percent ownership of Case.

Pryce Davies, struggled to improve spark timing and the carburetor performance.

J. I. Case entered the 1890s manufacturing center-crank steam traction engines. In 1895, Walrath's factory sluggishly turned out 126 engines of all types: skid, portable, and traction. Anticipating the production of gas engines, Walrath may have let the machinery age and facilities slip. The shops were small and too antiquated to

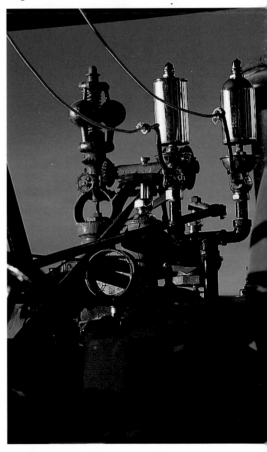

George Morris' other great idea was to mount the rear of the traction engine on coil springs and parallel arms. This softened the impact of abrupt road surface changes by supporting the rear axle independently from the boiler, firebox, and engine. Parallel arms allow the axle to rise or fall but always keep contact with the gears.

Case introduced the side-crank spring-mounted steam traction engines with 10 or 12 horsepower in 1895. By the time this 1913 40-horsepower model (number 29057) was produced, gasoline traction engines were as popular as Case plant manager Jesse Walrath had predicted they would be. Case produced its last steam traction engine, an 80-horsepower model, in September 1924.

engines. The board had selected Walrath's replacement already and hired Morris on March 22, 1897. His 1897 annual order, issued to him as newly named superintendent, included 50 Morris-type traction engines. He revitalized the shops to improve performance and increase output, and he dealt with suppliers and remedied quality problems. Within the year, Case named him general manager.

A new batch of engines appeared in September 1897, but they were no longer called Morris engines. They had side-mounted steam engines as the Morris did, and they used many Morris parts. They were identified as side-mounted engines, known in Case notations as "side-crank" or "SC" engines, in contrast to Case's previous center crank. Morris' shops finished the first one, number 6727, on September 3, 1897.

A greater modification appeared 12 days later. Morris mounted the engines on springs to reduce stress on the outer shell of the boiler, lessening risks during travel or plowing. This extended boiler life. Case completed its first SCSM steam traction engine, as they became known, on September 15. New engines in other sizes and configurations appeared, establishing the basic design that Case followed until it ended steam production in 1926.

The new traction engines encountered sales resistance at first. Some customers canceled orders; however, Morris' design quickly gained acceptance. His reorganization and improvements in the shops improved quality. He introduced new metals and methods. Case's prices

remained stable while engine power increased. The shops met orders easily and more followed. Case began outselling the industry; production jumped from 211 in 1898 to 920 in 1899.

Morris created larger engines primarily for plowing, including a new 20-horsepower size (later known as the 60-horsepower), which proved to be Case's most popular model. Case introduced a 110-horsepower model, and it built perhaps as many as seven 150-horsepower "Road Locomotives" for hauling applications.

Reborn after the failures of boisterous gas traction engineers, Case—and George Morris—combined effective factory management with new technology. Bringing the two together, Walrath was there at the launch of what historians refer to as the Golden Age of American Agriculture, from 1897 through 1914. It was a period of expansion, growth, and profit for all involved. Walrath was not wrong in his instincts or motives. In fact, his thinking was ahead of his time. He was just unlucky in his choice of gas engine builders.

This all coalesced to make Case steam traction engines a success. The company manufactured some 35,737 steam traction engines, more than twice what second-place Geiser produced. Part of this resulted from the company's early experiments in gas power. Case planned to manufacture 1,000 Patersons in 1895 but produced little more than 100 steam tractors. Had this gas engine proved itself, America's best-known steam engine would never have existed.

1904 Hart-Parr 22-40

H art-Parr wasn't the first company to produce and sell a gasoline traction engine. Charles Hart, Charles Parr, and their marketing manager, Walter H. Williams, were not the first people to use the word *tractor* in print. They weren't even the first company to advertise gas traction engines. So why were they important?

They were the first company to succeed in the tractor business as a tractor company. They had the benefit of a steadily growing economy in which science and technology proved to be farmers' friends. During this time, Hart-Parr entered a machine that could go out into a field and plow, or disk, or perform other tillage operations. Theirs was the first gasoline traction engine that did more than belt work (spending the entire day linked up by belt to a threshing machine).

Previous companies, some of which dated back to the 1880s, had tried producing gasoline traction engines. Some achieved some mechanical success, but none of the others stayed in the business. John Froelich in Waterloo, Iowa, produced a single-cylinder traction engine in 1892, using a Van Duzen engine. J. A. Hockett of Sterling, Kansas, produced simple sturdy machines as early as 1893. In 1898, Edward Huber manufactured and attempted to sell 30 of his single-cylinder models, and Harry M. Wallis advanced technology somewhat further with his enormous "Bear" in 1912. Still, each maker sold no more than a handful. Larger companies with vast steam traction engine manufacturing experience, most notably Owen Kinnard and Albert Haynes of Minneapolis, fabricated a few prototypes for their Flour City line, but they waited for technology and the marketplace to mature.

This 1904 Hart-Parr Model 22-40 was Hart-Parr's second production series, larger and more powerful than the first 17-30, introduced in 1903. The larger tractor offered not only a transport transmission to pull threshing machines, but also a heavy version with gears strong enough to plow.

Make-or-break ignition fired the spark only when the engine load required it. Hart-Parr used its own design, a horizontal two-cylinder engine, to develop 22 drawbar and 40 belt pulley horsepower at 280 rpm.

Enter two collegiate engineers with vision. Charles W. Hart and Charles H. Parr first met as engineering students at the University of Wisconsin at Madison. They quickly discovered a shared interest: internal combustion engines. Before long their ideas and experiments outstripped the rest of their class. They produced several experimental gas-powered engines in 1895 while still in school. They wrote a thesis that the engineering department published in its own magazine. Two years later, in 1897, while nearby J. I. Case was recommitting its efforts to steam, they formed a company to produce small stationary engines for the farm market. Hart was the idea man of the pair. Parr, four years older, created engine drawings as part of their study curriculum, and they used other engineering students who worked in the university machine shop to build and test larger experimental engines. It's more than likely Hart and Parr began developing their own tractors while still in Madison.

The stationary engine business grew to such an extent that they needed to expand their small facility. They wanted additional land for outside storage, most useful for aging iron castings. Property near the university was not cheap, however, so they approached a number of potential backers. Unfortunately for the two engineers, their timing was flawed; Madison was in the midst of a well-organized campaign to beautify the city. That would not include a new engine works. Hart's father, in Charles City, Iowa, offered financing provided his son brought his business home. Hart and Parr began construction of their new factory in early July 1901 and paid their first payroll on November 25, although some work continued in Madison into early 1902.

There is no way to know whether Hart-Parr began to manufacture its tractor in Madison or Charles City, but the company completed the process in Charles City in 1902. They sold this and their second tractor to local farmers, and they closely watched their machines' performance. Hart and Parr judged the tests a success, and in 1903 they began small production runs in two sizes of tractors.

The first production batch was the Hart-Parr 17-30. These models had a transmission suitable for transport only, and the tractor was intended for belt work. The third Hart-Parr produced (and now the oldest known surviving model) is owned by the Smithsonian Institution. Hart-Parr produced 17-30s in small numbers for another few years.

The second model, the 22-40, was larger and more powerful. These were similar to the 17-30s, but Hart-Parr offered them with two different transmissions. The same light-duty, transport version from the 17-30 was

Fred Schneider bought this 1904 model new in May 1905 and drove it home from the sales agency. Since that time, it has remained in the Schneider family, passed down to Schneider's grandchildren, Bill, Kim, and Will Paterson. It is the oldest known Hart-Parr in private hands.

A "homemade" radiator used exhaust routed up through the center to cool the huge engine. Hart and Parr devised a centrifugal pump to circulate engine oil through the engine and radiator. A friction clutch engaged forward or rearward motion. Reverse used a planetary gear cluster.

the standard equipment, but the partners introduced a heavy version, strong enough for plowing in 1904. Hart-Parr dropped the lighter gearbox in 1906. The company continued the 22-40 until 1907, when the output rating was increased to 22-45 by replacing pushrod-type valve gearing with rotary valves. These were in production until 1911. At that point, the company again strengthened and improved its large machine. Its output reached 30 drawbar horsepower and 60 on the belt pulley. This model was so consistent and dependable that it earned the nickname "Old Reliable" soon after introduction in 1911.

Hart-Parr's tractor production grew faster than the factory, which was constantly under construction trying to keep up. Hart and Parr discontinued stationary engines in 1904 after about 305 were manufactured. Word of their success spread, and several competitors launched serious challenges to the Iowa makers.

Hart-Parr didn't invent the word *tractor*. Historians know that Chicago inventor George H. Edwards used the term in his 1870 patent application, long before Hart-Parr's advertising manager took the word as his own. And Hart and Parr certainly were not the first engineers to produce gas traction engines; however, the range and quality of their models gave them a place in history. They were the first ones that mattered.

Steering was state-of-the-art, devised directly from contemporary thinking in steam traction engines. A slack chain wrapped around a worm-gear-driven shaft (also called a "fifth-wheel chain" steering system) tugged one end of the solid axle while allowing the opposite end to move forward.

The 1911 Rumely OilPull 15-30

The OilPull was a new product from Rumely, an old company that had long emphasized quality, and that is exactly why the OilPull is so highly regarded today. It was probably the best tractor of its generation. In an age of hype unmatched even in recent times, it lived up to its promise. OilPulls have been legendary ever since. It was the difference in performance and reliability between Rumely's machines and others of the era that changed mechanized farming forever. It dramatized the experience of Nebraska educator and state Senator Wilmot Crozier, who bought a Ford tractor built in Minneapolis and named after the company's accountant, Paul Ford. That poorly designed tractor failed on the way home from the dealer. Buying an OilPull to replace it and finding it far exceeded its maker's cautious claims was a revelation to Crozier.

American farmers, enjoying a growing economy that steadily fattened their wallets, were willing to trust what scientific experimentation could teach them. Science applied to technology, especially where it might protect their wallets, was a welcomed advance. The Nebraska Tractor Tests, mandated by the state legislature and performed by the state university at Lincoln, held every maker to its claims. Although the last OilPulls were built in 1931, some OilPull tractors remained in service into the 1980s on a ranch in Texas that pumped its own crude. Today, at the places where the truly old tractors gather, chances are good that you'll see more OilPulls than any other heavyweight tractor.

This is a 1911 Rumely OilPull Model E 30-60. The M. Rumely Company of LaPorte, Indiana, introduced its first OilPull tractor in early 1910. Independent designer John Secor created an engine that burned low-grade fuels, putting some in production in 1895. Rumely's factory superintendent, W. H. Higgins (Secor's nephew), perfected a carburetor that improved Secor's engine. The OilPulls became legendary.

Rumely introduced the two-cylinder Model E in 1911. With a bore and stroke of 10x12 inches in each cylinder, Rumely rated the big engine at 30 horsepower on the drawbar and 60 on the belt pulley at 375 rpm. This was extremely conservative. In Nebraska tests, the Model E tested at 49.9 drawbar and 75.6 pulley horsepower.

At the turn of the twentieth century, gasoline was expensive. The only gas at that time was naturally occurring casing-head gasoline, a by-product of the refinery processes. This was something not yet specifically sought after. The wave of internal-combustion use that swept the country—this was the era of Henry Ford's affordable Model T, and soon after, the introduction of the motor truck—caused the price to skyrocket (relative for the times, at least). Kerosene was plentiful, although it was more difficult to burn. It was harder to vaporize; as liquid fuel, it leaked past cylinder rings into crankcases. This diluted the lubricating oils, and the result was higher engine wear.

Rumely's engineers specifically designed their engines to burn kerosene, but innovatively. Instead of cooling with water or air, as others did at the time, Rumely used oil as the coolant. This permitted higher engine temperatures that vaporized the kerosene better. The OilPulls didn't introduce oil cooling, but it was one part of their package.

Early experimental OilPulls were not especially successful. Dr. Edward A. Rumely, whose grandfather founded the firm in 1857, demonstrated the OilPulls for other companies, hoping to entice them to purchase his designs and patents. The competition was unimpressed when they watched raw fuel running out of the carburetor. It took outside talent, the proverbial "hired gun," working with a creative insider, to straighten out the tractor and especially the carburetor.

John A. Secor, the outsider, had an interesting background. He had played with combustible heavy fuels since the 1870s, when he experimented with a boat propelled by fuel explosions under the keel, a sort of early jet boat. Later, a shop engine that he built to drive the line shaft in the boat shop turned into a thriving business. His nephew, William H. C. Higgins Jr. already worked for Rumely as factory superintendent. Higgins designed a carburetor that mixed kerosene vapor and air better, an important advance. Both men shared ownership of the carburetor patent, while Secor held several other patents on his own.

Dr. Edward Rumely came back from medical school and other travels through Europe, during which time he met inventor Rudolf Diesel. Going to work in 1908 for the family company, he proved himself in his first task by wooing Secor to Rumely's offices in LaPorte from his own New York business. It wasn't the Rumely Company's first attempt to attract Secor, but this time the doctor succeeded. Secor and Higgins designed the first OilPull, a machine nicknamed "Kerosene Annie," with assistance from Rumely's steam engineers. They used many Rumely traction engine parts. Secor and Higgins refined carburetors for the OilPull that vaporized the kerosene and also injected water into

the mixture to reduce pre-ignition, or "knocking." Kerosene has a very low resistance to pre-ignition (where the compression of the heated piston ignites the fuel before the spark can do so). A method of controlling this was vital in a tractor that relied on high engine temperatures to aid vaporization. (Pre-ignition puts tremendous strain on pistons, connecting rods, and crankshafts while also burning valves.)

The Secor-Higgins tractor was efficient, durable, and powerful at a time when competitors often were not. Although other companies caught up with and

then surpassed the Rumely OilPull in technology and performance, the OilPull established a reputation for quality that endures.

The Rumely Company didn't endure, however. It stuck with the OilPull through the 1920s, when it was clearly outdated. The Great Depression drove the final nails, and in June 1931, Allis-Chalmers purchased Rumely, mainly for its dealer organization and distribution system. Rumely's LaPorte, Indiana, plant would soon be manufacturing Allis All-Crop combines, a harvesting machine milestone in itself.

This was neither a small nor an inexpensive machine. It weighed 13 tons, stood 19 feet long, 13 feet tall, and it sold new for $4,300. That's approximately $85,000 in today's dollars if you adjust for inflation.

The 1913 Waterloo Boy One-Man Tractor

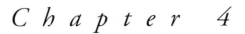

The Waterloo Boy tractor is fondly regarded today as the ancestor of John Deere's two-cylinder tractors and the beginning of its regular production tractors. But while Deere collectors revere Waterloo Boys as the great progenitor, it's worthwhile to recall how the tractors and their side-by-side two-cylinder engines came about. In the beginning, there were people with ideas. America's healthy economy encouraged responsible business owners—and irresponsible entrepreneurs alike—to enter the farm technology marketplace. The individual with many ideas, one who gave several tractors their life, was Harry W. Leavitt. Leavitt moved around the Midwest, designing tractors and patenting his ideas. The patents were issued in his name, although evidence suggests he was often working for others who, at this time, remain unknown. He devised direct-mounted implements before nearly anybody else, receiving patent number 990,993 (for which he applied on March 14, 1910) while living in DeKalb, Illinois. He applied for a crawler-tread patent, number 1,112,460, on April 12, 1912, after moving to Paris, Missouri, although he actually completed and signed the application in Waterloo, Iowa. (He apparently even completed a crawler prototype with the Waterloo Gasoline Engine Company in 1913.) Another crawler with direct-mounted implements followed on June 12, by which time Leavitt had relocated to Waterloo. The tractor drawing shows clearly it used a four-cylinder upright engine.

In 1912, Waterloo Gasoline Engine Company introduced its first Standard 25-horsepower tractor with a four-cylinder vertical, transverse engine. By 1914, Waterloo switched its production models to a horizontal two-cylinder in both 15-horsepower "Light" and 25-horsepower versions. This 1913 Waterloo Boy Model R is the earliest-known 25-horsepower Model R.

however, it switched to smaller models with two-wheel drive and opposed cylinders.

Louis W. Witry had worked with Waterloo Gasoline Engine Company since the 1890s. He did much of their stationary gas engine development. When Waterloo got into the traction engine business, it was natural that Witry also got involved. Although his patents on the chassis were few (a sliding side-hill hitch and a steering apparatus), his involvement with the engine was great. Witry patented the horizontal two-cylinder, side-by-side configuration that later would make John Deere famous. His motivation for changing from the opposed engine was that two cylinders together required a shorter run for exhaust to warm a single carburetor and less distance for the vaporized fuel/air mixture to reach the cylinder. This simple configuration allowed better performance on kerosene.

The resulting Waterloo Boy Type RA (introduced at a 12-24-horsepower rating in 1914 as the Model R) and Type RN tractors (manufactured from 1917 through 1924 and known only as the Model N) were moderately successful in their sales. They were anything but perfect. Deere & Company engineers examined the competition and noted that Waterloo Boy tractors were neither powerful nor reliable. One Deere plow dealer who sold Waterloo Boy tractors had resolved to stop selling them because he became fearful of the damage they were causing his reputation. Deere's designers theorized that a Waterloo Boy should pull more than one 16-inch sulky plow and maintain reliability, as engineer Theo H. Brown recalled in his *Deere & Company Early*

Early engines used nonremovable heads, also known as "blind heads." The valves were mounted in cages. Designers Louis Witry and Harry Leavitt placed the oiler on the manifold using a single cream bottle. Waterloo introduced the removable head on its H series that first appeared in 1916.

In April 1913, Leavitt applied for a patent for what appears to be an opposed two-cylinder Waterloo Boy. The application also featured a three-point implement hitch some years before Irish inventor and promoter Harry Ferguson ever saw a tractor. By this time, Leavitt had returned to Paris, Missouri, although, as earlier, he completed the application and signed it in Waterloo.

Some interesting general purpose, single front-wheel-drive tractors followed. Then Leavitt patented an all-wheel-drive tractor using the previous single-front-wheel configuration he coupled to convention-al, driven-rear wheels. He applied for both of these patents in late 1913 from Iowa. Leavitt was advancing technology. A gypsy for some of his life, he settled in Waterloo and went to work full-time for the engine company. When Waterloo Gasoline Engine Company started production, it began by building large tractors and crawlers. Soon afterward,

Rear spokes were round on early series Model R tractors, and the guide band around the front wheels was later revised. Waterloo stamped the engine serial number only on the end of the crankshaft. If a farmer with an early tractor rebuilt the engine and replaced the crank, the tractor took on a later serial number.

Tractor Development, recently reprinted by the American Society of Agricultural Engineers (ASAE).

By the early teens, Deere's board of directors came to believe the company had to get into the tractor business in order to continue to sell its plows. The previous decade was financially rewarding, but this period was even more encouraging. The cost of farmland was rising as more Americans wanted to leave cities. New farmers needed plows and, in these progressive times, they might choose a tractor instead of horses. Deere tried one prototype designed by experimental engineers C. H. Melvin and Max Sklovsky, but tests between 1912 and 1914 were disappointing. The company encouraged board member Joseph Dain's ideas for an all-wheel-drive model in 1914. He continued development through mid-1918. In December 1917, the board approved a small production run of 100 of their homegrown Dain tractors to put them into farmers' hands for in-field development. But Deere needed manufacturing, foundry, and milling facilities for tractor production.

Deere's head of sales, Frank Silloway, led them to Waterloo, Iowa, to inspect a company he knew was available. They saw the facilities they needed and also a tractor, somewhat crude, but one already established

in production. They acquired the company and its tractor line in March 1918. The 100 Dains were not completed until 1919, by which time Case, Ford, International Harvester, and Rumely had a sizable sales advantage over Deere's expensive all-wheel drive. Deere needed the Waterloo Boy right away.

Then Waterloo Boy established a historical distinction on March 31, 1920. The Nebraska legislature required all manufacturers who wished to sell tractors in their state to submit them for testing at a newly established facility and test track on the state university campus in Lincoln. The first tractor tested, and the first one to pass, was a 12-25-horsepower Waterloo Boy N.

Still, despite Nebraska's acceptance of the tractors, the Waterloo Boy's quality problems combined with a changing tractor market. Theo Brown and Frank Silloway were concerned, but Louis Witry and Harry Leavitt had a new series of alphabetically designated prototypes ready to show them, each using a revised version of the two-cylinder engine that Witry had pioneered in the Waterloo Boys.

Earliest production models laid the fuel tank on its side and elevated it for gravity feed. Later production series enlarged the radiator and cooling fan and moved them to the left side of the frame. The mushroom-shaped tube at right is the crankcase breather tube and cap.

The Waterloo Gas Engine Company produced something like 8,081 Model R tractors in variations from letter A through M between 1914 and 1917. Almost half that production went to England, as the Overtime, for World War I food production.

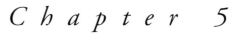

Best and Holt and Their Crawlers

F lotation, or weight distribution, was a big problem for early tractor makers. The powerful steam traction engines were heavy and most of that bulk rested on tall, narrow rear wheels. This weight brought down bridges designed only for horses and wagons, and in fertile river bottomlands, such as the San Joaquin River valley of central California, it sunk the machines into soft soil or mired them in sand. For that, a continuous track, or crawler, was the solution. This spread the machine's weight over not just two small wheel patches but along two frames wrapped in long, wide tracks. In California, Daniel Best went head-to-head against Benjamin Holt to provide large, powerful, steam traction engines for farmers who worked the fertile deltas.

For these two old-line manufacturers and their competitors in the Midwest and East, gasoline power provoked even more controversy than the usefulness of crawlers. By 1906 and 1907, Hart-Parr and International Harvester had gas traction engines in production and the marketplace seemed interested. Manufacturers such as Rumely, Buffalo Pitts, Geiser, and Kinnard-Haines tried their hands at it. So did Best and Holt, but Owen Kinnard quit when he encountered opposition from rail companies that refused to load his gas engines on the same cars with threshing machines. Ben Holt established Aurora Engine Company to go outside his own organization because most of his stockholders distrusted the fuel. Building the tractors required little new technology, however.

"All that was required," historian Reynold Wik wrote in his book *Benjamin Holt and Caterpillar*, "were changes in blueprints and building and mounting of gasoline motors on existing chassis

This 1917 Best Tracklayer turned out 75 horsepower. Clarence L. Best and Benjamin Holt were fierce competitors in the crawler market. Both produced powerful machines meant for farming in sandy or spongy soil throughout central California. Despite constant feuds over patents, both machines were remarkably similar.

Holt steered its Caterpillars using the patented track clutches and brakes, while the front tiller wheel helped bring the nose around. Best used track brakes and a large differential on its Tracklayers. This enabled Best to keep power on full throughout a turn but meant the long crawler couldn't turn as tightly.

Both Best and Holt built their own engines. This Best 75 four-cylinder 7.75-by-9-inch engine turned out 82 horsepower at 500 rpm. Holt rated its four-cylinder 7.5x8-inch engine at 75 horsepower at 550 rpm. Exhaust came straight out of each engine and the noise, while under load, was thunderous.

[designs] which had previously carried the boilers of the steam traction engines. . . . The new industry was launched almost full-grown."

Holt had his first gas-engine Caterpillar crawler in field tests as early as December 1906. At least three of the first six production models joined Holt's huge steam crawlers already digging in the Mojave Desert to bring water to Los Angeles, an area of struggling orange groves destined to raise more people.

Despite a 1908 purchase agreement where Ben Holt acquired Daniel Best's company (and prohibited Dan's son Clarence from any tractor production for 10 years), Clarence founded C. L. Best Gas Traction Company. In California, land prices were increasing as unsuccessful miners discovered the state's next gold crop was wheat. The company that Dan Best sold to Holt made 50- and 110-horsepower steamers; now C. L. manufactured gas-engined 70-horsepower crawlers, ignoring the terms of the sale. Each of these machines stuck a single, wide wheel far out front. This steering, or "tiller," wheel also helped balance the elongated machine. He started making the 70-horsepower in 1912, and then refined it into a 75-horsepower tractor that he introduced in 1914. During this same time he also produced several models with traditional round rear wheels.

The rivalry between the two makers continued with a vengeance. Best called his machines "Tracklayers," while Holt registered his name, "Caterpillar," as a trademark in 1910. He had crawlers as early as 1908, and introduced his tiller-wheel 75-horsepower crawler in 1917. They looked similar, but mechanically they were significantly different.

Philip Rose, technical editor of *The Country Gentleman*, a farm journal of the day, toured tractor makers during 1914 and 1915 to learn who made what and how well. Billy Durant, the founder of General Motors who feared competition from Ford's announced tractor, paid for Rose's research. (Durant wanted to buy an existing company. Rose, in his final written report, ultimately steered him to Samson.)

"Best," Rose declared, "has developed many refinements which have been thoroughly proved out, while Holt sticks to the old conservative design, always trying to improve their materials and methods but not changing or adding to the mechanism."

Rose examined Best's drive system and Holt's, which "drives each side separately and eliminates the differential," he wrote. "Best has a huge differential, which enables them to pull just as hard around a corner as on the straightaway. They can outpull a Holt anytime on a corner." Both tractors were steered by applying power, and, by now, both had brakes on each track. "It's not necessary to use the hand [steering] wheel at all

except on a straight road. On a crooked road, it is much easier for the driver as he merely has to move a little lever back and forth to steer." Of course, under plow load (each was capable of dragging eight-plow gangs) the traction of the crawler tracks and the torque of the engine raised the front wheel high above the ground.

It wasn't long before Holt's chief engineer at the Peoria, Illinois, plant, Bill Turnbull, questioned the need for that front wheel. Turnbull created a wheelless Holt 45-horsepower crawler for the 1914 Panama-Pacific Exhibition in San Francisco. He demonstrated the crawler on a platform, spinning left and right, its front end light enough to float once it lacked the extra weight of that wide wheel and steering mechanism. Philip Rose had even seen a prototype, developed by mechanical engineer E. F. Norelius, who worked for Holt at the time. Rose reported that Norelius was experimenting with a "two-tread" machine Holt introduced in 1916 as the Caterpillar 45.

"It is steered," Rose wrote, "by throwing the caterpillars [tracks] on each side into or out of gear. This machine is not catalogued, but it sells for $3,000. I understand that they turned out only a few of this type for this country but that this was the type which was made to order and sold to Germany for their guns long before the war." Best, without military contracts to produce hundreds alike, continued throughout the war to update and improve its home-market crawlers.

Although Germany, and later the United States and its allies, used Holt 75s and six-cylinder 120s to tow cannons into war, it wasn't too long before other inventors tried mounting the guns on armor-plated crawlers, thereby creating a milestone of another type, the military tank.

Both Best and Holt provided power steering on their large crawlers. Here, Best used a chain-driven pump from the front engine pulley. Holt's system was nearly identical. The front tiller wheel on each machine was nearly 2 feet wide and 4 feet tall, and the assembly weighed more than 1,400 pounds.

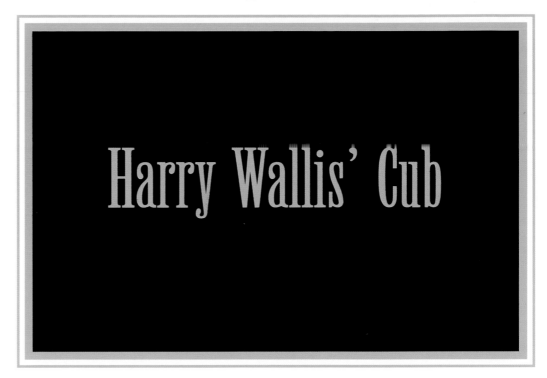

Harry Wallis' Cub

S team traction engines had one characteristic that governed basic layout. Nearly all had their engines mounted above their boiler. Gearing that connected the engine to the wheels traveled down alongside the boiler. This could not be enclosed because boiler heat would complete whatever damage normal friction began. Open gears ran cooler, but they were exposed to dust and rain, destroying what lubrication survived the boiler heat. Some makers tried canopies over the entire tractor, but these provided poor protection.

Designers who had simply replaced boilers and steam engines with gas engines discovered the problem. Steam boilers were the strong frame that kept mechanical parts rigidly in place relative to one another. Without that boiler, gas tractors needed a frame. Early experiments used steel channels that, even when bolted or riveted together, were prone to flex and wear.

The advent of affordable automobiles with small components suggested an answer. Most cars had transmissions that ran in rigid cast-iron cases constantly lubricated by oil contained inside them. For tractors, Cyrus McCormick effectively pioneered the idea with the Auto-Mower that engineers Bert Benjamin and Edward Johnston created for the 1900 Paris Exposition. Johnston fit running gear into Benjamin's cast-iron mower frame, submerging moving parts in oil. Subsequent inventors cited McCormick's Auto-Mower in numerous patents as the true forerunner of integral frame tractors.

This 1914 Wallis Cub was a revolutionary improvement. It influenced the next generation of tractor design, and it affected the configuration of farm tractors right up to the present day. Designer Robert Hendrickson solved the problem of keeping dust out of the engine and keeping lubricating oil in with his rolled sheet-steel trough.

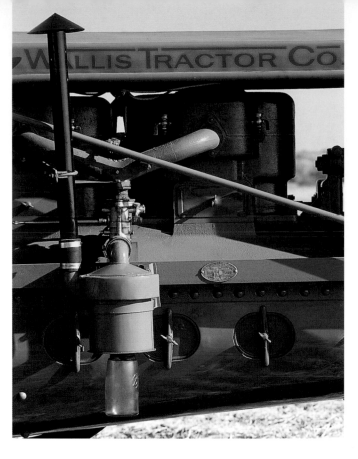

The idea surfaced next in Dearborn, Michigan, with Henry Ford. He had enclosed hundreds of transmissions in cast cases in his automobiles. In 1910, Ford assigned engineers Joe Galamb, Richard Kroll, and Jimmy Smith to build something stronger than the frail Model T–derived tractors they had tried so far. They created a 5,000-pound machine using a 50-horsepower four-cylinder engine mounted horizontally and transversely. The crankcase and transmission supported the front axle and radiator without additional framework. Patented in 1912, this is probably the first integral frame tractor, but it was too large and heavy a machine. It was going opposite to what Ford wanted. He stopped further development after the prototype. Harry M. Wallis came next.

Based in Cleveland, he had two talented men creating his tractors, Robert O. Hendrickson, his chief designer, and Clarence M. Eason, his chief draftsman and later assistant chief engineer. Hendrickson's first work for Wallis was the Bear, a conventional frame, 100-horsepower, heavyweight sod-busting tractor that he designed in late 1912. But in January 1913, before Wallis even built the first Bear, Harry knew it was too large a machine for the market. Fifty years earlier, the Homestead Act of 1862 had opened the Great Plains to farming and the space committed to this purpose doubled in the next 40 years to 839 million acres. But once big steam power and later large gas engines had opened the soil, the big machines were almost useless in the second season. While Wallis started to manufacture 10 Bears, he devised a successor to continue this line of tractors: After the Bear came the Cub. While the name was similar, mechanically it was altogether different.

Hendrickson and Eason started with traditional elements, front-wheel steering turntable, engine, transmission, rear end. They fit these in one single heavy sheet-steel frame rolled into a U, a structure Hendrickson called "trough-like." They riveted and caulked in steel plates to form compartments for the engine, transmission, and

Hendrickson and his assistant, Clarence Eason, conceived an engine, transmission, and final drive rigidly mounted within a seamless U-shaped enclosure. Inspection ports allowed farmers access to connecting rods, crankcase main bearings, and other internal mechanisms, yet the steel housing also supported front and rear axles.

This unified system that served as framework for the tractor and enclosure for the mechanical elements became known as unit-frame, or unitized, construction. Harry Wallis carried it through his subsequent Cub Jr. models and subsequent designs, even after Massey-Harris acquired Wallis and J. I. Case Plow Works in 1928.

A large tractor by later standards, the Cub was not only startling for its unit-frame construction but also for its compact size. Wallis' previous model, the Bear, was nearly 20 feet long and twice as heavy as this Cub.

Massey-Harris, which acquired Harry Wallis' tractor operation in 1928, carried over Robert Hendrickson's unit frame until it introduced the Model 30 in 1947. Hendrickson's design caused Henry Ford's engineers Joe Galamb and Joe Farkas to recall a prototype they'd done for Ford, and to apply the idea to their new Fordson.

final drive. This U-frame provided a rigid enclosure that kept dust out of the tractor and oil in; it maintained all moving parts in proper alignment, which reduced wear, increased efficiency, and gave the industry a new standard to measure itself with. IHC's Ed Johnston worked on a similar idea as Wallis' designers completed their prototype. (Johnston's 20-40 Mogul was semi-unitized; its front wheels hung off a frame rail extension.)

Hendrickson didn't directly connect the engine, transmission, and final drives to the frame. Wallis hired Walter Carver to design a new 60-horsepower engine to fit this unusual configuration. As a mathematician, Carver also calculated stresses to the U-frame and recommended adding parallel Z-bar along the top for additional torsional rigidity. They found they could mount individual elements to this structure, and Carver's engine bolted in place. They made each part into a compact subassembly. These could be withdrawn in one piece after removing only a few bolts. This eased maintenance and overhaul and sped up manufacture. Unit-frame construction swept through the industry, reaching IHC before coming back to Ford. Following Ed Johnston's prototype 20-40 Mogul with its modified unit frame, IHC used this technology on its McCormick-Deering 10-20 and 15-30 tractors.

Wallis' Cub was a moderate sales success as well as a technological innovator with Carver's water governor and four-lobe cams and Hendrickson's live axle. After completing the first 10 Cub prototypes in the spring of 1914, Wallis continued to produce them for six years, manufacturing about 660 in all. (The prototypes had the fuel tank mounted over the front wheels; regular production placed it behind the engine.) While the Cub was about half the size, half the weight, and half the price of his earlier Bear, it was still a large machine. Trends were leading makers to even smaller tractors. (Wallis followed up with his Cub Jr. With that model—half the price, weight, and size of the Cub—sales multiplied.) Once Wallis completed the first 100 Cubs, he and his son Mitchell relocated all production to J. I. Case Plow Company in Racine in November 1914. Case Plow merged with Wallis in 1919. Then in 1928, Canadian implement-maker Massey-Harris acquired Case Plow. Massey-Harris needed tractors to fill out its line. The unit-frame Cub and Cub Juniors influenced Massey's tractor engineering, and the basic design remained in production through 1945 in its Challenger and Pacemaker models.

The 1918 Fordson

When it came to tractors, Henry Ford's only competition was the horse. It wasn't shortsighted arrogance; he sympathized with the farm owner whose place was too small to use a big Rumely or Case and had to walk behind animals all day. He knew there were about 1,000 tractors in use in 1910, but that number jumped to about 25,000 by 1915. He also understood that for every farm with a tractor, there were a hundred using draft animals. Ford's goal was to produce something small, strong, and affordable. To do that, he needed to manufacture tens of thousands of them. Those kinds of tractor plans made his shareholders nervous. To escape their hassles, he and his son, Edsel, established Henry Ford and Son, and called the machine they produced the Fordson.

Following years of testing Model T–based prototypes and a unit-frame horizontal four-cylinder prototype, Ford's chief engineer Joe Galamb suffered a case of déjà vu during the summer of 1914. A visiting parts salesman showed him pictures of Harry Wallis' new unit-frame Cub, for which designers Robert Hendrickson and Clarence Eason received a patent. It reminded Galamb of Ford's 1910 unitized experiment, also patented. But Hendrickson's version came closer to Ford's goals of light, strong, and easy to manufacture. Ford immediately stopped experiments on Model T tractors, and Galamb's assistant, Joe Farkas, got a new assignment. Farkas had labored mightily to produce an efficient worm gear final drive for Ford's experimental electric car, built mostly to honor Ford's friend Thomas Edison. The car failed, but the final drive soon crossed disciplines and

This 1918 Fordson was partially inspired by Robert Hendrickson's radical unit-frame design for the Wallis Cub. It caused Ford engineer Joe Galamb to recall a 1907 50-horsepower prototype he'd constructed. The engine crank and gear case supported the front axle assembly and rear wheels as well. Galamb and engineer Joe Farkas designed a three-piece enclosure derived from their 1907 prototype and Wallis' ideas.

An entrepreneur in Minneapolis, William Baer Ewing hired an accountant named Ford so he could use the well-known name on his own product, a tractor of dubious ability. With the name registered and Henry Ford's own board upset by costly tractor experiments, Henry named his machine the Fordson, incorporating son Edsel in the company and the product.

Henry Ford intended his compact, maneuverable tractor to replace farm draft animals. He didn't even consider other tractor manufacturers as his competition, believing there were enough farmers still using animals to create a huge market for all makers. His vast Rouge factory near Detroit allowed enormous output, which reduced costs and gave birth to a great tractor marketing war.

replaced Ford's favored planetary transmission as the rear end of choice. After solving the problem of reducing speed by splitting that duty between the transmission and the worm, friction was the next challenge. Farkas and Galamb inverted the worm, bathing it in oil, eliminating wear and heat.

Joe Farkas convinced Ford's manufacturing boss Charles Sor-ensen that their tractor needed no frame. Farkas could design castings stout enough to support the entire tractor. They finished the first prototype in an early snowfall in November 1915. They tested it and built more, ultimately 50, each a hand-built, mostly unique machine, through 1916. The advent of World War I in England pushed things rapidly.

Charles Sorensen traveled to London, looking for a place to build the tractor in the United Kingdom to help reduce their food shortages. Former Ford automobile distributor Percival Perry was appointed to the Food Production Board. Perry knew the British Board of Agriculture and the Ministry of Munitions (MoM) intended to mass produce tractors and lease them to farmers (since every available Englishman and horse were needed in Europe). He

proposed they select the Ford, but when bombing raids destroyed some of Sorensen's preferred sites, Ford suggested they build tractors in Dearborn and ship them to England. The Royal Agricultural Society of England examined Henry's prototype and admired his production record with his popular Model T cars and trucks. They designated his machine the official MoM tractor and ordered 5,000. Ford agreed to sell them for $50 over cost, or $750. The government had decreed that all grass—parks, lawns, golf courses—was to be plowed up and planted.

Once MoM's order was set, Ford heavily revised the tractor. Farkas had created separate castings for engine, transmission, and rear end. Ford reconfigured the whole tractor into two, one for the engine and steering assembly, the other as the entire drive gear line, with the transmission and rear end preassembled and slid into its large casting.

While Ford geared up manufacturing for MoM production, England still needed tractors. Dozens of entrepreneurs already produced conversion kits for Model Ts, and they raced into action. Most notably, the St. Paul, Minnesota, manufacturer E. G. Staude shipped 10,000 of its $225 Mak-A-Tractor conversion kits, distributed as the Eros Tractor for use on the Model Ts already there.

Ford then accepted an order for 1,000 MoM tractors from the Canadian Food Board in Ottawa, Ontario. The U.S. government established county war boards aimed at making equitable use of limited resources. Most agricultural states were allocated 1,000

tractors, and most of them wanted what England and Canada were getting. As American distribution began, Ford became concerned about the implements working behind his tractor. He arranged through the War Production Board (which International Harvester's president, Alex Legge, led) to borrow IHC's implement master, Bert Benjamin, to develop compatible tools. This was no altruistic loan of a senior executive. IHC needed assembly line production, and it was unconvinced that high-speed automotive-type engines would work in tractors. By the time Benjamin left Dearborn when his work was done, he had as many answers as he'd provided Sorensen and Ford.

As Ford did with others of its products, Henry kept Fordsons in production too long without improvements or updates. His goal was noble: provide a tractor for every farmer who could afford one. But this goal had problems and shortcomings. When demand dropped, he cut his price, redefining the word *affordable*. The Fordson sold more copies than any other make, and for several years it outsold all the others combined. Henry's low price, possible through the economies of his monstrous River Rouge assembly plant (where ore arrived on ships at one end and tractors drove out the other), brought many old-line giants to their knees in the early 1920s. The Fordson taught the rest how to survive. Bert Benjamin and Alex Legge took pleasure in its eventual defeat.

It was an extremely simple machine. George Holley, the Bradford, Pennsylvania, machinist who had devised a carburetor for Henry's Model T automobile, created his Model 234 for the tractor. The intake and exhaust manifolds intertwined to aid fuel vaporization.

The regular production Fordson engines placed the oil filler at the front of the block. This was unlike prototypes and the earliest production versions built for Ford by Hercules—about 1,000 in all—where the filler was at the rear. The Auto-Synchron Spark Box provided ignition.

35

The 1921 International Harvester 15-30 with Power Take-Off

The power take-off, or PTO, is as old as the tractor itself. In California, steam traction engine manufacturers—and bitter competitors—Dan Best and Ben Holt linked their engines to huge wheat harvesters they towed behind, with flexible connections and steam lines to power the auxiliary steam engine that operated the entire harvester. The principal appeared earlier, when steamers pushed chain-driven binders and mowers in England and Europe. Prepared for the Paris Exposition of 1900, both Deering and McCormick Auto-Mowers used solid mechanical connections to drive machinery. The familiar rear-mounted, external revolving shaft first appeared in central France in 1906 where inventor/farmer Albert Gougis used it to drive a McCormick binder through downed grain.

In America in 1907, Transit Thresher of Minneapolis, Minnesota, used a similar shaft between the Transit 35-horsepower four-cylinder gas traction engine and the thresher. Designer D. M. Hartsough conceived the system. This would move this rig through the field, threshing shocked grain instead of bringing the shocks by wagon into the farmer's yard in the traditional manner. While Gougis' invention worked, the Transit Thresher application was less successful. None of these ideas caused any imitation in an industry often driven by copycats. The machines and ideas mostly faded away—but not entirely. And certainly not in the mind of IHC engineer Ed Johnston, who, upon reading about Gougis' creation, and then getting an invitation from the inventor, traveled to France to see it.

International's 15-30 and smaller 10-20 models incorporated the design improvements of Wallis' Cub and the Fordson with International's own full-length unit-frame construction. IHC found an additional benefit to the unit rigidity; alignment of its drive gears allowed IHC to develop and introduce power take-off (PTO).

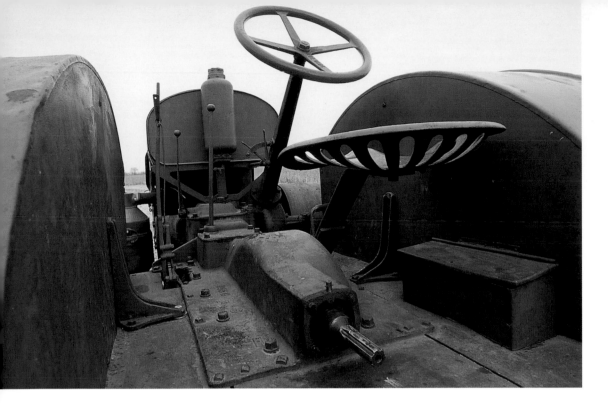

IHC first tried power take-off on the 8-16 in the spring of 1919, but its parallel rail frame twisted too much. In late September 1920, Tractor Works authorized prototype 15-30s with PTO, and the next February it approved the apparatus as an option. International's 15-30 became the first tractor tested at the University of Nebraska that was fitted with a factory PTO.

Standard-tread 15-30 models with the optional PTO created panic among manufacturers who had committed to transverse mounted engines, such as Deere & Company and Case. While that configuration got power to the rear wheels more efficiently, it meant PTO shafts needed more complex engineering.

Their memories came in handy in late September 1917. Benjamin, an implement designer for IHC's McCormick Works, was in the fields in Napanee, Indiana. A wet summer interfered with the hemp crop harvest there. Benjamin went to watch three IHC hemp binders work. He wrote back to Chicago that the harvesters' IHC engines choked and were ruined by the

dust and straw kicked up in dry conditions by the tractors that pulled them. He saw the nose-heavy harvesters sink in soft soil. He also saw duplicate fuel consumption when both harvester engines and tractors took on distillate. Benjamin suggested using the tractor engine to supply power to the binder.

His letter sparked activity throughout IHC. Several engineering departments began work on the idea. The first successful PTO application that IHC sold was an International 8-16/binder combination, marketed together as a "Tractor Binder." IHC specifically stated it was "not constructed to be drawn by horses." Farmers bought a few of them, but the power take-off was definitely added on, and the combination was expensive. It was a moderate engineering success, and Benjamin and Johnston believed it had potential.

Early International 8-16s had several problems. Now competition from the Fordson (and a strong postwar economy still supported by Europe's inability to feed itself) gave impetus to a Tractor Works' program in 1920 to design lighter, more powerful, more reliable—and more rigid—tractors. Integral frames provided rigidity, all-enclosed drivelines improved reliability, and ball-bearing crankshafts enhanced power. These new four-cylinder 15-30-horsepower machines (and soon after, a 10-20 counterpart) proved to be extremely durable, and they became very popular tractors. But the 15-30 had one enduring claim to fame: It was the first tractor sold in the United States that was designed from the start to have a PTO.

IHC sometimes promoted the new gear-final-drive 15-30s using the advertising slogan "Triple Power," referring to the drawbar, belt pulley, and power take-off. IHC also went the next big step. Bert Benjamin designed numerous implements for the new tractors. Binders, mowers, manure spreaders, and combines, among other machines, appeared from IHC's factories, each driven by its new PTO.

Competitors scrambled to produce tractors with power take-off, but it was not an easy engineering feat. Earlier design and manufacturing decisions had led makers such as Case and Waterloo to mount engines cross-wise to more easily get engine power to drive wheels. Other tractor design configurations put engineering obstacles in the way of running a shaft out the final drive. But now, just two years later, it got more difficult.

The U.S. economy began to tighten following World War I, as Europe could once again feed and clothe itself. Few makers had resources to invest in new development. Worse, after the world war had ended, Ford created a tractor sales war that forced price cuts on companies barely able to stay afloat in the tightening money market.

IHC's design linked the PTO shaft to the tractor's main drive. When farmers disengaged the clutch, interrupting power to the drive wheels, the PTO shaft stopped as well. This "dependent" PTO technology eventually improved with the development of an independent PTO shaft, with its own clutch, a configuration that young Ed Johnston had actually introduced in 1900 with McCormick's Auto-Mower. International Harvester's power take-off drove not only a new kind of implement, it also drove the competition to redesign its machinery. By the 1930s, nearly all the manufacturers offered tractors with available PTO.

To make full use of the power take-off, IHC engineers devised a shifting hitch mechanism that allowed the farmer to properly align the towed implement to the PTO shaft. International Harvester promoted the 15-30s, calling them Triple Power Tractors, meaning drawbar, belt pulley, and the new PTO.

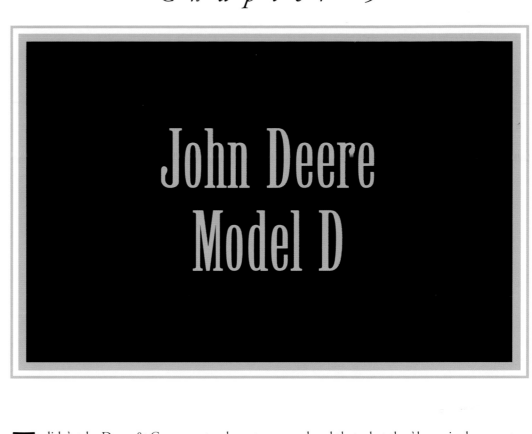

John Deere Model D

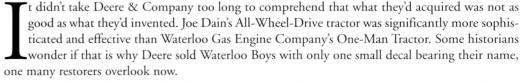

It didn't take Deere & Company too long to comprehend that what they'd acquired was not as good as what they'd invented. Joe Dain's All-Wheel-Drive tractor was significantly more sophisticated and effective than Waterloo Gas Engine Company's One-Man Tractor. Some historians wonder if that is why Deere sold Waterloo Boys with only one small decal bearing their name, one many restorers overlook now.

Deere's head of sales, Frank Silloway, had introduced his management to Waterloo, and he led efforts to acquire the facility and its product. As a result, he and chief engineer Theo Brown were first to examine what they'd bought. They learned that Waterloo's two engineering wizards, Louis Witry and Harry Leavitt, had already conceived the replacement. Knowing they must retain its most expensive element, the horizontal two-cylinder engine, they let their imaginations run free.

Witry and Leavitt showed Brown and Silloway plans for seven prototypes, some they had already assembled. Fond of alphabetical labels, Leavitt started over with Style A on these prototypes. This model was smaller than the current Waterloo Boy Model N. Leavitt shortened its wheelbase, and Witry reversed its horizontal engine on the frame, orienting the crankshaft to the rear. They reset the chassis closer to the ground.

Brown and Silloway encouraged them to continue. As each major improvement or design correction changed the tractor significantly, Witry and Leavitt went to the next letter, building seven Style B prototypes, then seven Style C models. By now, they reduced the weight from 6,200 pounds

When Deere & Company acquired Waterloo Gas Engine Company, it knew it got a working, marketable farm tractor in the Waterloo Boy. It didn't know that Louis Witry and Harry Leavitt had already started designing its replacement. By reversing the Waterloo two-cylinder engine, they created their own unit-frame model.

to about 4,000 pounds, and shortened the tractor from 132 inches overall to about 109 inches. Improvements in carburetion, intake and exhaust valves, manifolds, and engine bearings increased drawbar horsepower from 16 to 22.5 from the same engine block. Convinced they'd achieved the best version, they assembled a single prototype Style D tractor and, in 1923, approved it for production. And that took real guts.

Competition among tractor makers was fierce, nasty even, since Henry Ford entered the fray. Harry Wallis had produced a unit-frame Cub tractor reminding Ford's engineers of an earlier design of theirs. Ford put all the financial might of his company behind his Fordson, making it a formidable challenger to Wallis, Case, International Harvester, and Deere's dated Waterloo Boy. Other makers offered four-cylinder engines, yet here was Deere still running its horizontal twin. By mid-1922, when Deere director Leon Clausen suggested still more Style C prototypes be built, Waterloo had manufactured 786 tractors the year before but sold only 79. Production for 1922 called for just 307 Waterloo Boys. Was this any economic environment to develop and introduce a new machine? Clausen's answer was emphatically yes. He had statistics: There were now more than a quarter million tractors on American farms, 60 times as many as a decade before.

"There is a national demand for tractors," he told the board. "We do not have to create it. When a suitable

The first production run of spoked-flywheel Model D tractors used a large 26-inch-diameter wheel. This remained in production through 1923 and 1924, about 879 in all, before Deere reduced the diameter to 24 inches in late 1924. Deere printed operator's instructions on the fuel tank wall.

The first Model D tractors operated from the left side of the platform, opposite of the Waterloo Boy tractors. Deere kept the left-side steering until 1924, when it recognized that the steering column was too close to the flywheel, and it substituted a jointed steering rod.

tractor is built at a reasonable price to the consumer, it can be sold." Price was still a major consideration. Ford pressed his tractor price war. International Harvester pushed back (and others tried) in an economy collapsing under postwar Europe's agricultural recovery.

Deere's Model D, as the Style D became known, was in fact a suitable tractor at a reasonable price. After a slow start, sales took off. But Theo Brown and Louis Witry refused to sit by idly while other manufacturers continued their own improvements. The first 50 Model Ds appeared in 1923 with a welded front axle and left-side steering. The flywheel, used for starting the D instead of a crank as other makers did, was a 26-inch-diameter six-spoked wheel that Witry bolted onto the driveshaft. Beginning with the 51st tractor built, Deere substituted a stronger cast front axle. At the start of 1925, they fitted a heavier 24-inch-diameter spoked flywheel, and a year later they keyed a new solid flywheel onto the drive shaft. Confident now of its new machine, in 1926 Deere & Company renamed the Waterloo operation the John Deere Tractor Company.

From the start, Witry broke new ground. In his patent application covering nearly the entire Model D tractor, he described his intent "to provide certain improvements by which the construction of the tractor will be simplified and cheapened without detracting from its efficiency or strength." "Cheapened" referred not to quality but to manufacturing costs. Taking pages from his competitors' battle plans, he'd created a unitized frame tractor for assembly on Waterloo's first-ever production line.

Not content to be last into battle—or least equipped—once its contender was ready for market, Deere stretched the envelope further. Engineer Harold E. McCray created a power take-off system, running independently through its own clutch, which he patented in November 1928, though Deere did not put it into production. But the world economy had its own plans and in late October 1929, when the stock market crashed, it opened a huge financial wound that bled American industry's creativity. Healthy companies hunkered down, cut expenses, slowed research, and simply tried to hold on. Dozens of manufacturers and thousands of farmers left their businesses. Wall Street may have needed something like Deere's live PTO to drive the world out of its economic pit; however, once things began to improve and outlooks brighten, other engineering developments idling along from 1929 through 1933 emerged.

Recognizing the limits of the two-cylinder power plant, another Deere engineer, John T. Liggett, created a torque-amplification system. This he patented in 1934, as a device he called a "gear reduction transmission" by which "tractor speeds are somewhat reduced to produce a corresponding increase in drawbar pull of the tractor." But economic recovery was still slow, and the Liggett torque-amplifier had to wait. And wait. When it appeared again, it was International Harvester that introduced it in 1954 after Liggett's patent expired.

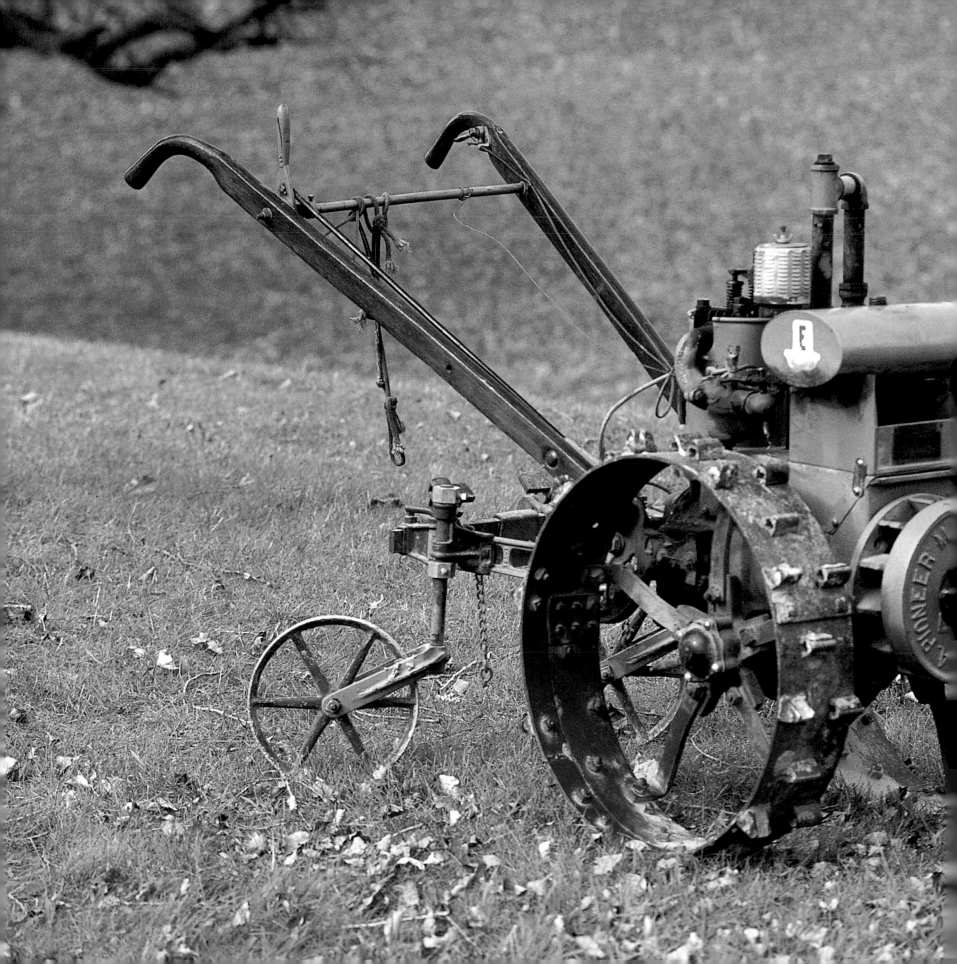

Garden Tractors

During the late teens, three significant trends moved on farm tractor manufacturers and farmers. The first was the widespread introduction of motor trucks and their subsequent heavy promotion by periodicals such as *The Chilton Tractor Journal* and, to a lesser extent, *Agrimotor*. Editorials boosted their importance; technical articles explained their value to farmers. By 1919 the New York Motor Show, which in previous years had shown trucks on the same floor with automobiles, decided that year to give trucks (and tractors!) their own exclusive exhibition for a week immediately following the automobile show. Outside midtown Manhattan, the periodicals pushed their second discovery.

Chilton and *Agrimotor* devoted reams of paper to cultivating tractors. Stories on individual makers led up to *Chilton*'s April 1919 multipage overview titled "Big Field for Cultivating Tractors in Row-Crop Work." In subsequent issues, they featured Heider, Toro, Avery, International, Case, Indiana, Boring, and other models. In June 1920, however, on the other end of the farm equipment spectrum, there appeared an equally well-publicized phenomenon: 14 pages on "Baby Tractors: Small in Size but Big in Possibilities." These odd-looking machines appeared to be the result of a mating of a single-cylinder stationary gas engine with a wheelbarrow frame or a hand truck, connected to a miniaturized disk harrow. They were called garden tractors for a simple reason: Most tractors in production at that time—with some exceptions—were nearly the size of a small garden.

This 1922 Red E Power Cultivator was produced by MBM Manufacturing of Milwaukee, Wisconsin. The Red E was "designed to perform the work of four men or one horse." Weighing 425 pounds and meant to cultivate from 100 to 250 feet per minute, it sold new for $250. The rear caster wheels regulated cultivation depth. By the late 1930s, Pioneer Manufacturing took over production and offered pneumatic tires.

Case and other old-line makers still produced steam traction engines and would for another few years. Even the Fordson or International Harvester's radical new 8-16 was barely capable of maneuvering in the spaces most farmers set aside for their kitchen garden. *Chilton* estimated that by mid-1920, 14 makers would produce 35,000 garden machines that year. Often, the manufacturers had women running these machines at demonstrations, stressing their ease of starting, operating, and maneuvering.

The baby tractors were available in two sizes, a larger, two-cylinder model that could plow and usually weighed 600 pounds to more than 1,000 pounds, and smaller versions at 250 pounds meant for cultivating and golf course mowing. Manufacturers such as

MBM fitted its Power Cultivators with its own single-cylinder 4.5-horsepower engine largely derived from Fordson and Ford car parts. Bore and stroke were 3.75x4.0, and it used a small Holley carburetor and Bosch high-tension magneto. It was 73 inches long and just 17 inches wide. Red E produced several models in the 1930s, with Zenith carburetors, ranging from 2-horsepower walking models to 7.5-horsepower riding versions.

R. H. Sheppard was an unflappable devotee of diesel engines and designed and produced this single-cylinder 5.4-horsepower air-cooled model for use on his smallest model ever. Its tires were 4.00x12 inches in front and 7.5x16 inches in the rear. It sold for $1,095.

California, home of C. L. Best and Ben Holt and birthplace of Caterpillar crawlers, also yielded the Pull-Away Tractor. It was manufactured in Holt's hometown, Stockton. First manufactured by Fred Lewis using Wisconsin engines, these crawler garden tractors were sold mainly in the San Joaquin Valley. The last 50, of which this is one, were produced by Capp Brothers of Stockton, using a Briggs and Stratton motor.

This is a 1946 Rototiller Model HG Power Gardener. The next year, Rototiller Inc. of Troy, New York, advertised this "Roto-Ette" as the "all-purpose Power Gardener." Originally a sheet-metal shroud covered the cultivating tines to protect operators' feet. Rototiller used Briggs and Stratton 1.5-horsepower gas engines. The company was owned by Graham-Paige Motors, which produced sleek stylish automobiles

Macultivator, Tillermobile, Consolidated Engine Company (makers of the "Do-It-All" cultivator), Beeman (which made the One-Horse Tractor for cultivating), Midwest Engine Company (which produced the "Utilitor" for cultivating or mowing), Hurst ("Small Garden Tractor," cultivating), Atlantic Machine ("Merry Garden Tractor" for cultivating), Homestead Tractor (the "Auto-Tiller" for a 10-inch plow), Edfield ("Universal," plowing), New Britain (a $450, two-cylinder, 6-horsepower plowing model), and others soon found more serious competition.

Oldsmar, makers of a 5-horsepower, single-cylinder, 1,000-pound "light-duty tractor" plowing machine, was introduced at the 1920 National Farm Equipment Show. It was designed and backed by Ransom E. Olds who had earlier tried his hand at manufacturing an Oldsmobile Tractor.

Chilton's writer, H. E. Everett, interviewed Harry B. Smith, a progressive dealer in Anderson, Indiana, who sold both full-size tractors and the new small models.

"We saw there are a lot of farmers owning two- and three-bottom tractors who kept a horse or two merely to do some of the light work around the farms. We knew of farmers using a one-horse plow for getting into the corners of their tractor-plowed fields, or for getting up close to the trees in an orchard." Smith was an enthusiast, but as Everett wrote, he "sells [garden tractors] as a supplementary source of power capable of doing efficiently some of the smaller farm operations for which larger tractors are not economically practical. He regards it more as the long-wanted source of power that makes the motorization of the farm complete."

The "baby tractor" market evolved, as did its full-size cousin. In the early 1920s, new manufacturers appeared that produced much smaller, lighter machines, weighing less than 200 pounds and capable of work only in family gardens. Robert Kinkead, who had designed the Bull and Little Bull tractors a decade earlier, brought out a $190 one-wheel cultivating machine on which the small, single-cylinder engine fit inside its single wheel rim.

H. C. Dodge (in New York City) introduced its Sprywheel 135-pound $150 machine, boasting that one gallon of fuel provided one day's work. In late 1922, MBM Manufacturing of Milwaukee introduced its Red E Power Cultivator, "designed to perform the work of four men or one horse." The 425-pound Red E, introduced at $250, boasted a low center of gravity, aided by its two caster wheels at the rear that "enable the operator to devote more time to operating the tractor" rather than balancing it. Red E remained in business into the early 1950s. Another automaker joined the market in the mid-1940s, having also produced full-size farm tractors a decade before. Graham-Paige Motors Corporation in Willow Run, Michigan, manufactured the stylish Graham-Bradley tractor that it sold for a while through Sears, Roebuck and Company catalogs. It watched the garden tractor business for some time before acquiring a small Tryo, New York, company founded in 1930. The company produced a well-built product called the Roto-Ette. When Graham-Paige took over, it wisely renamed the machine for the company it bought, establishing a trademark that to this day identifies all similar products as clearly as Kleenex is a facial tissue and Xerox is a photo copy. Graham-Paige called its 450-pound machine the Rototiller.

Copar Panzers were manufactured in Pennsylvania. They were known for their quality of assembly and durability, which made them among the first lawn and garden tractors to become collectible. If quality and durability is a function of weight, the Panzer's attributes are obvious if you've ever pushed one. Distribution centered along the east coast but this one escaped to Wisconsin.

Starting in the late 1950s, many full-line farm equipment manufacturers entered the lawn and garden tractor business. This provided them off-season sales and service opportunities for dealers facing slow activity during those periods. Some manufacturers bought existing smaller companies. Others, such as Minnie-Mo, IHC, and Deere manufactured machines from scratch in under-utilized factories. The third option was to buy "off the shelf" products from small makers who would paint and decal "to order."

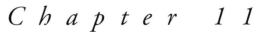
International's 1924 Tractor for All Purposes

Tractor manufacturers were headed in the right direction. Harry Leavitt's Waterloo One-Man Tractor promised farmers machines capable of field chores without needing an assistant. Harry Wallis' Cub, Henry Ford's Fordson, and Ed Johnston's McCormick-Deering 15-30 furthered technology with unitized construction. Each did better at keeping the dirt out and oil in moving parts, and each was smaller and lighter than machines manufactured even five years earlier. Yet none was suitable for the delicate, precise work of row-crop cultivation.

In late 1915, Ed Johnston's assistant, David Baker, completed IHC's prototype Motor Cultivator, a machine he, Johnston, and chief implement engineer, Bert Benjamin, hoped was suitable. After only two years of production and improvements, they learned it was not.

Bert Benjamin, while disappointed, was not discouraged. Soon after IHC dropped the Motor Cultivator, Benjamin took his new ideas to Johnston, who assigned Philo Danly to design tractors for Benjamin's implements.

Collaborating with Baker on early efforts, Danly and Benjamin mounted a Waukesha engine lengthwise on the tractor frame ahead of the single steering wheel. This immediately improved the balance. Danly adopted a differential with sprockets and chains driving widely spaced front wheels. They devised an automatic turning brake. Baker fitted a reversible operator's seat and a three-speed forward-and-reverse transmission.

The Farmall grew out of International Harvester's experiments and production of its Motor Cultivator in 1916 and 1917. The idea of a cultivating tractor was growing in popularity, a natural evolution after the downsizing from International Harvester's prairie sod-busting Titans and Moguls to smaller, lighter machines.

International Harvester's Gas Power Engineering carried over automatic turning brakes from its Motor Cultivator. Prototypes went from "heavy" versions in late 1920, known as the "Farm-All" through many changes, to a "lightweight" named Farmall by May 1921.

Johnston, needing a designation for this new project in late 1919, asked for suggestions. Tractor Works secretary Ed Kimbark proposed "Farm-All." By early 1920, as Benjamin completed designing its implements, the name became Farmall.

This Farmall got little support outside its three designers. Johnston was too busy finishing new 15-30 and 10-20 gear drive tractors to welcome another configuration. Although it evolved from his Motor Cultivator, the Farmall was not his idea. What's more, IHC's powerful sales department proposed a new steam tractor as gasoline prices rose sharply in Canada and the western United States (and in response to reliability problems with its 8-16). The ongoing post–World War I agricultural depression slowed tractor and implement sales; Motor Cultivator losses depleted money available for hand-built development models. Danly, Baker, and Benjamin completed their first prototype, using an L-head IHC truck engine from Akron Works, in early February 1920. The second came on June 30, using the engine

that carried on through to production even though the tractor evolved considerably.

The biggest change came around Christmas 1920. Tractor Works had completed five prototypes for Benjamin. He determined they could perform 11 farm operations while IHC's International 8-16 could do 4. Yet some IHC officers felt Farmalls were too heavy. One of Benjamin's engineers, C. A. Hagadone, sketched a version weighing about half that of the 4,000-pound prototypes.

This "lightweight Farmall" differed in other ways. It ran in only one direction, pushed now by its two powered "rear" wheels. It steered with a single front. Tractor Works enclosed final drive housings and another Benjamin assistant, Arnold Johnson, moved the cultivators forward to straddle the front wheel. This allowed farmers to steer rapidly, to cultivate without damaging crops. This "enhanced dodging facility," he said later, was a turning point. The Farmall still faced an uphill battle. Alex Legge, elected IHC president in June 1922, supported it, but as a frugal Scotsman, he encouraged additional development.

IHC's executives frequently discussed the Fordson. In 1917, as Henry Ford prepared for U.S. distribution,

Because Ed Johnston and Bert Benjamin derived this tractor largely from the Motor Cultivator, it did not adopt the unit-frame construction of the earlier gear-drive 15-30 and 10-20 McCormick-Deering standard-tread tractor. Meant as a cultivating tractor, visibility and maneuverability in row crops were its primary goal.

he approached Legge (who also served as chairman of the wartime U.S. Food Production Board) for help designing implements. Legge knew Ford used automotive-type engines in the Fordsons, assembling them on high-capacity production lines. Legge may have felt IHC had much to learn from Ford. He dispatched Bert Benjamin to Dearborn. Ford concluded implement production was not beneficial. Benjamin learned production lines could assemble automotive-engined tractors efficiently, knowledge that IHC quickly applied to its own plants.

By mid-1922, Benjamin was frustrated with battling executives and other engineers. According to IHC historian C. W. Gray, Benjamin issued "an ultimatum that he must be given free rein" on the Farmall. While there is no evidence that Benjamin contacted Ford or engineers Joe Galamb or Gene Farkas with whom he'd worked in 1917, he may have hinted to Legge that he might change jobs. Legge quickly named him assistant to the chief engineer of International Harvester, overseeing all Farmall development.

Tractor Works completed 26 preproduction models by August 1923, another 100 by February 1924 for field testing, and 200 more as "limited trial production" by September. Some executives worried that Farmalls would kill sales of 15-30 and 10-20 models, but Farmalls went into the cotton-growing southern states where IHC's standard-tread tractors never had succeeded. Finally, in late March 1925, a showdown of

sorts occurred. Houston branch sales manager Jim Ryan told P. Y. Timmons, IHC's manager of tractor sales, that if IHC didn't produce the Farmall, "we'll organize a company in Houston and build it here."

IHC set Farmall production at 2,500 tractors for 1926. Good crop harvests in late 1924 made farmers ambitious for 1925. They ordered 15-30 and 10-20 models and asked about Farmalls. IHC opened its Farmall Works in Rock Island, Illinois, and sold 4,430 Farmalls in 1926. They produced 9,502 in 1927 and 24,899 in 1928. Competition from Ford's Fordson, which had forced dozens of manufacturers out of business, finally did in Ford itself. The tractor war taught IHC how to produce and promote its machines against competitors. Ford discontinued Fordson manufacture in the United States in 1928, shifting assembly to Cork, Ireland. Starting November 1929, Ford imported 1,500 Fordsons a month, while Rock Island built nearly twice that, totaling 35,517 that year. IHC became America's dominant tractor maker.

On April 12, 1930, IHC manufactured its 100,000th Farmall and 42,093 that year. Two months later, Tractor Works turned out its 200,000th 10-20 Gear Drive. But in 1931, the agricultural depression, made worse by the 1930 drought that destroyed crops, caught up with what started on Wall Street in 1929. Farmall sales collapsed to 14,093 for the year. IHC still held the lead, but the market had convulsed. And other tractor makers were working hard too.

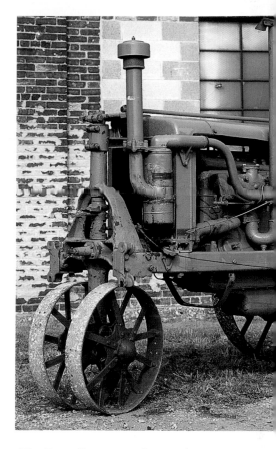

The Farmall represented not only a farm equipment advance, but it also caused fierce political bickering within IHC engineering and management. The company's executive committee wanted to make certain it was reliable and only slowly increased production until an IHC branch manager in Texas threatened to organize his own company to build it himself.

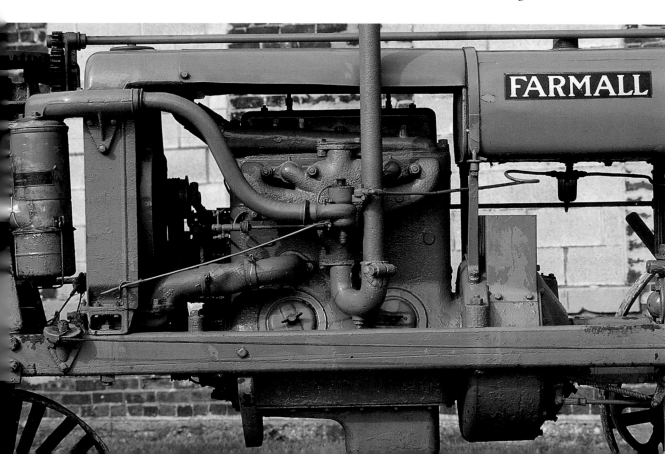

This is a true milestone, not only for the significance of the Farmall tractor but for the importance of this particular machine. This is QC-503, the third production-series Farmall manufactured and the first one delivered into private hands. It lived all its working life in Iowa. International Harvester reacquired it in 1945, and it has remained in IHC and Case-IH hands since then.

Chapter 12

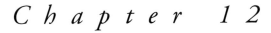

Case 1930 Model CC
Row Crop

F ew observers dispute that International Harvester's Farmall was significant when it appeared in 1924. Yet three years earlier IHC had used its overweight, overpriced, unbalanced, and underproduced Motor-Cultivators to send Case, Ford, Deere, and its other competitors on a wild goose chase. IHC showed its Farmall experimental tractors at a demonstration in 1921. The others also saw IHC's awkward, backward-running, motor cultivator–derived "heavy" Farmalls. Ed Johnston's Tractor Works tested these before adopting Bert Benjamin's lightweight style that they put into production. Case (and Ford and perhaps others) began testing similar concepts in the early 1920s. Case experimental chief R. B. Coleman rushed the company's own motorized cultivator into existence in 1922. Deere conducted unsuccessful experiments before this. Each of these makers dropped these ideas after concluding, like IHC, that they were unstable, complicated, expensive to produce, and they lacked versatility. Several aftermarket companies produced row-crop conversions for Fordsons with some success; they also introduced the sliding wheel on the rear axle. Everyone took notice.

Deere was the first to put a tractor into production in 1928 to compete with the Farmall. Deere's design engineer, Louis Witry, and engineering chief, Theo Brown, conceived their GP, or General Purpose, row-crop model to work three rows at once. The response from IHC was a none-too-subtle chuckle. Case was next to introduce a factory-built row-crop model. Case's vice-president of engineering, David P. Davies, was worried that farmers might agree with Deere's vision, so he and chief engineer Robert O. Hendrickson designed a three-row–capable machine. (Hendrickson had

The Model CC—or C-Cultivator—was Case's row-crop version of its Model C standard-tread tractor. It was conceived as a smaller cultivating version of the Model L. Introduced on steel wheels in late 1929, by 1934 buyers could select pneumatic rubber for an additional $70, compared to $1,025 for all steel in 1931.

55

Chapter 13

Massey-Harris 1930 General Purpose Four-Wheel Drive

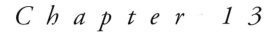
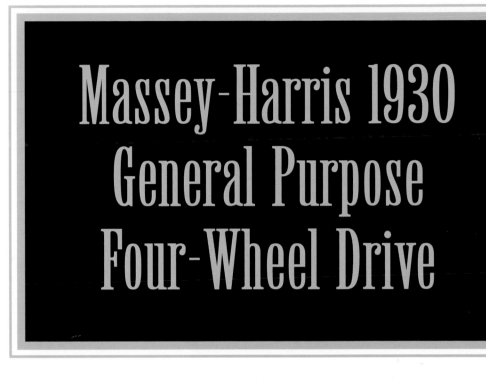

I t was such a good idea that nobody even knew they needed it yet. By April 1930, when John Rodgers applied for his patent on a four-wheel-drive agricultural tractor, the concept of general-purpose row-crop tractors was still a novelty, even though *Chilton's Tractor Journal* had featured his machine a decade earlier. And four-wheel drive? Well, that was much less unusual.

As early as 1911, buyers could find four-wheel drive. Morton Tractor Company of Fremont, Ohio, produced an opposed two-cylinder 25-horsepower model. A year later, Morton collaborated with Heer Engine Company, in nearby Portsmouth, on the Morton-Heer 25-horsepower. In Great Falls, Montana, the Olmstead Gas Traction Company tried for about a year. Samuel S. Morton in Harrisburg, Pennsylvania (not related to Morton Tractor in Ohio) had much greater success. He sold his first company to Ohio Manufacturing as the foundation for International Harvester's friction-drive tractors. Then he produced several four-cylinder, four-wheel steering "tractor trucks" into the 1920s when he merged with Pennsylvania Tractor Company in Philadelphia. They manufactured Buda four-cylinder, 40-horsepower models and a monstrous six-cylinder model that sold for $5,000.

By 1920 the market had even seen three-wheel drives. Joe Dain had produced a three-wheeler for Deere & Company, in development from 1914 through 1918, and Wharton Motors in Dallas, Texas, manufactured its 3WD 12-22 with a four-cylinder Erd engine. International Harvester's Ed Johnston built a number of prototype four- and six-wheel-drive tractors on the International 8-16

Massey-Harris' sales brochure explained that this new four-wheel-drive tractor, with all four wheels of the same diameter, "provides constant contact with the ground and assures balanced traction at all times and under all conditions." Massey's engineers created this innovative machine about 25 years before farmers were ready for it.

Using an enormously complicated system, Massey-Harris' front wheels transferred power out to the wheels before dropping it down to the axle hubs. This allowed designer John Rodgers to maintain the highest ground clearance, something like 30 inches to the bottom of the axle, and the widest row width by using the long king pin.

For reasons unknown, Massey used a 226-cid Hercules engine for the GP four-wheel drive. This engine tested at Nebraska and developed 19.9 drawbar and 24.8 belt pulley horsepower. Aware of complaints that the GP was underpowered, Massey got a new overhead-valve Hercules engine and rubber tires in 1936. This tractor, number 35008, was the eighth 1936 model produced with the larger engine.

rail-frame platform. No fewer than 12 manufacturers across the United States offered four-wheel-drive models for sale. Yet, by 1928, they were gone, victims of the postwar economic downturn, Henry Ford's tractor war, and the growing fascination with tricycle-configuration row-crop and cultivating tractors. As every other maker withdrew, Massey-Harris' John Rodgers was working on his. And it certainly wasn't effortless.

Massey-Harris had attempted to enter its Canadian markets for tractors by importing and distributing D. M. Hartsough's Big Bull tractor in 1917. When this tractor failed to meet their expectations, Massey management converted their Weston, Ontario, plant to manufacture Dent and Henry Parrett's 12-25 Model E. Massey labeled this its Massey-Harris No. 1. The Parrett's successive improvements became Massey No. 2 and No. 3. But this tractor and the licensing arrangement also dissatisfied the Canadians who ended their agreement with Parretts in 1923.

About that time, J. I. Case Plow Works Company considered acquiring some or all of Massey, because the Canadian government threatened to raise import tariffs. Case then could say it was a Canadian manufacturer. This led to violent arguments within Massey-Harris, leading the Massey family to sell its interests. While this made running the company easier, it still left M-H without a tractor. The company's relationship with Case Plow was intact, so in 1927 M-H acquired rights to sell Harry Wallis' Model OK 20-30 tractor throughout Canada and parts of the United States. Massey then purchased Case Plow in 1928 for $1.3 million, quickly reselling the Case name to the Threshing Machine Company for $700,000. For its $600,000 investment, M-H got Case's Racine, Wisconsin, address, Wallis' tractor, and other

Case projects already in development. Tariffs no longer mattered. Massey put its engineers to work with Hendrickson to improve the Wallis, creating for 1929 the new Certified Model 25 (guaranteed to produce 25-drawbar horsepower—it developed 26) and a smaller 10-20. Massey, aware of International Harvester's Farmall and John Deere's GP models, also absorbed extravagant development costs while John Rodgers labored in the back shop.

His was an idea poised for a comeback using a design he'd thoroughly tested. Massey-Harris was pleased. Its first new tractor would be something radically different from everyone else's: Its semi-unit construction had four-wheel drive, it used automotive-type steering, and its axles pivoted in the middle to keep all four wheels flat on the ground no matter what terrain the operator used. Unfortunately, its Hercules

four-cylinder engine suffered power losses through Rodgers' highly complex driveline and the tractor developed only 15.9-drawbar horsepower. Then the stock market crashed, and the economy permitted no farmer or company to embark on anything so radical. Even in a healthy economy, it was just too different.

Massey-Harris had operations in Europe that were even larger than what it ran in North America, and its Depression-era losses worldwide threatened to destroy the company. There was no money available to develop a more powerful tractor engine. Rodgers received his patent on his four-wheel-drive general-purpose tractor in late 1933. Massey's losses, in the millions, became so serious that Massey's directors voted in January 1935 to liquidate the company business in the United States and Europe (except for the United Kingdom), returning to a tight nucleus of operations in Canada only.

But just as this happened, M-H brought home to Toronto its former European sales manager Jim

Duncan. Duncan balked at Massey's doomsday plan. He insisted to the board the worst was over in Europe and the United States as well. Financial reforms and increased farm credit in America had begun to lubricate the machinery market. The board gave him one year. It gave Rodger's five-year-old GP4WD the same. In 1936 each got a reprieve. General product sales had turned around, and Rodger's GP got a new overhead-valve Hercules engine and rubber tires.

Sadly, the power increase was negligible, and at a time when the rest of the market was narrowing up the front end, Massey-Harris quietly let the GP4WD slip out of production in 1938. The company sold fewer than 4,000 during its life. It was a strikingly wrong idea introduced at the worst possible moment. When four-wheel drive appeared again, it was the only one in the market; however, Wagner Equipment in Portland, Oregon, gave its four-wheel drive plenty of power. It not only twisted in the middle of the tractor, it bent there.

Designer John Rodgers conceived this high-ground clearance 4WD as Massey-Harris' version of a row-crop cultivating tractor. This narrow-tread version was meant for vineyards and orchards. But the complex machines were underpowered and reached Massey dealers just after the stock market crashed.

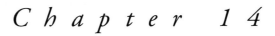

Caterpillar 1931 Diesel 60

The inventor didn't know what to call his new engine. He thought about the Delta engine, or maybe "The Excelsior." On paper he named it the "Rational Heat Engine on the Diesel Patent," but his wife said to him, "Just call it a diesel engine." So that is what he did.

Rudolf Diesel, a German born in Paris in 1858, conceived this engine while he was still a teenager, challenging himself to invent an internal-combustion engine that used compression to fire an air-fuel mixture. Making his dream come true required years of experimentation. In late 1893 his first experimental engine was ready. With a crude fuel pump injecting a petrol mixture into his cylinder, which generated 18 atmospheres (252 psi) of pressure, his engine fired at last. One time. The gauge atop the cylinder exploded from the pressure, scattering shrapnel around Diesel's lab.

Once he solved the problems and had a running diesel engine, he showed that his engine used one-third the fuel that Nikolas Otto's gasoline version needed to produce identical work. Several American engineers invited Diesel and his engine to the San Francisco World's Fair in 1915.

Diesel never made the trip. He was a psychological mess, troubled by his failures and plagued by the treachery of others jealous of his invention. Late in 1913, sailing from Germany to England to open an engine factory there, Rudolf Diesel leapt overboard and drowned in the North Sea.

Diesel was gone, but his engine lived on. One of them reached San Francisco, where it operated a generator in the Machinery Building near both Best's and Holt's tractor exhibits. Charles

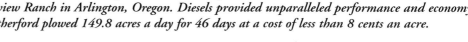

This was the 12th diesel-engined crawler Caterpillar sold, delivered to Mark Weatherford at Fairview Ranch in Arlington, Oregon. Diesels provided unparalleled performance and economy. Weatherford plowed 149.8 acres a day for 46 days at a cost of less than 8 cents an acre.

Caterpillar's huge 1,090-cid diesel had four cylinders of 6.125x9.25-inch bore and stroke. At its rated engine speed of 700 rpm, the crawler developed a maximum 65.1 drawbar and 77.1 PTO horsepower. In its lowest gear, the 24,390-pound machine could pull nearly 11,991 pounds at 2 miles per hour.

With such performance as the diesel produced for Weatherford, his children nicknamed the tractor "Old Tusko" after a large elephant they'd seen during a visit to the Portland Zoo. Operating on 16-inch-wide grousers, the crawler measured 101 inches wide and 161 inches long.

Manning, C. L. Best, and his chief engineer, Oscar Starr, came frequently to the city to examine the engine. Its economical operation convinced them some version of it should go into a tractor someday.

The engine also attracted the attention of George A. Dow, a pump manufacturer in Alameda, California (not far from Best's shops), and he obtained production rights from diesel's English makers. Dow produced 28 diesels, all three-cylinder, 150-horsepower engines for marine applications.

Dow also stayed in touch with the people at Best. When Best and Holt consolidated to form Caterpillar in 1925, the company brought in one of Dow's engineers, Art Rosen. Rosen had already envisioned diesel engines in crawlers and would play a key role in designing diesel crawlers for Caterpillar.

In the meantime, experiments by two other men who believed in diesel crawlers forced Cat's hand. Industrialist and steel-magnate Henry J.

Kaiser saw the potential of the diesel engines that John Lorimer produced for the Atlas Imperial Company, and Kaiser felt they should be used in Caterpillar's machines. In the mid-1920s, he visited Cat and expressed his ideas to Best, Starr, and Rosen. "If you won't put Atlas diesels in your Cat chassis," he grumbled, "I will!"

The Caterpillar folks politely declined, so Kaiser went ahead as promised. He had John Lorimer install Atlas diesels in Caterpillar and Monarch crawlers. Kaiser shipped three of these converted—but untested—crawlers to a Mississippi River project. There he discovered that stationary-type engines needed structurally rigid and environmentally controlled conditions. The heavy diesels destroyed the Monarch and badly damaged the Cat 60 chassis.

Challenged by the diesel engine's potential, and by its ability to shake his frame to pieces, C. L. Best threw his support behind a huge effort to make the combination work. In 1926, Best dedicated Caterpillar's research to diesels, spending $1 million before marketing one. Rosen and Starr designed the D-9900, Cat's first diesel.

Robert Bosch, maker of magnetos for airplanes, automobiles, trucks, and tractors, developed hydraulic injection for the fuel mixture into diesel engine cylinders. By 1927, Bosch's pump proved reliable, and Benz diesel trucks began shuttling throughout Europe. Bosch shipped one to New York in late 1927. Now in 1929 his pumps developed reliability problems so Cat built its

own, first using a group of German watchmakers to assemble them, and later, local housewives, when wartime sensitivities arose.

Best knew that starting techniques had to be made foolproof like the engine itself, or it would never sell. Caterpillar used gasoline "pony" engines almost from the start. The diesel's advantages, which Henry Kaiser understood earlier and better than most, became apparent. In 1932 gasoline for agriculture sold for 14 to 16 cents per gallon, whereas diesel fuel cost 4 to 7 cents per gallon. In early tests, Diesel Sixty prototypes performed well under heavy workloads yet consumed only 4 gallons per hour. Starr and Rosen still felt that close attention to early users was wise.

One of those early users was Mark Weatherford, the owner of Fairview Ranch in Arlington, Oregon. Cat sold him an early Diesel Sixty, number 1C12, in March 1932. Curious about its performance, he kept detailed records of his first work with the tractor. From March 4 to April 27, 1932, Weatherford plowed 6,880 acres with an Oliver 12-bottom, 16-inch plow. Weatherford calculated that 1C12 saved him $600 in fuel costs alone over his previous year with his 60-horsepower gas tractor.

Despite performance and economy, selling the diesel was tough. Everybody wanted to be third or fourth to buy one, but not the first. Stories like Weatherford's, moving slowly across the country, helped convince buyers of the power and economy. Cat sold more diesels in 1936 than in the previous four years combined. Production reached 1,000 engines a month.

Then real problems appeared with Cat's new machine: engine problems. Piston rings stuck, cylinder walls scored, and main bearings burned up. Art Rosen noticed that engines running West Coast oils—oils with a paraffin base rather than an asphalt base from the East—didn't experience piston rings sticking as much.

Caterpillar worked with Standard Oil of California to duplicate the West Coast oil. Rosen and Standard Oil engineer G. B. Neely collaborated to develop the first detergent oil that Standard named "Delo." Standard couldn't get it distributed, so Caterpillar put every dealer in the oil business, selling Delo all over the United States. The new oil solved the ring-sticking problem.

Gas and kerosene engine makers struggled against the diesel's economic advantage, ironic after Cat's fabulously expensive efforts to develop and perfect the power source. Through the 1930s, competitors held their own trials. International tested Hill diesels before introducing its own in its WD-40 in 1935. Other fuels came and went, but diesels steadily took over. The noisy clattering combustion became the official sound of farming throughout the world.

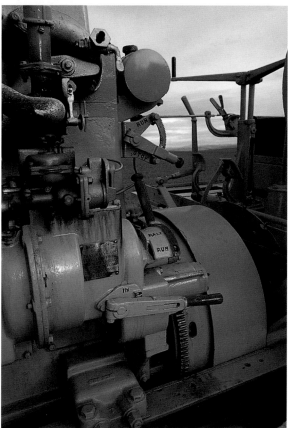

Caterpillar believed in the diesel and spent more than $1 million to bring the engine successfully into production. To be certain its customers were satisfied and that each diesel worked as the company anticipated, Cat sold its first dozen only to farmers it knew, at farms where careful record-keeping was routine.

Because diesel engines operate at such high-compression ratios to ignite the fuel without a spark plug, the usual compression-release methods of crank-starting gas or kerosene engines would not work. Caterpillar and many of those who followed used a two-cylinder gas engine to preheat the engine and crank over the diesel to start it.

1932 Allis-Chalmers Model U on Rubber Tires

Farm tractors rarely run on dry, smooth pavement. They're in the dirt. And not just one kind soil but in every variety, condition, and slope . . . Steam traction engines first rode on wooden wheels. But even hardened wood shattered when machines gained weight. Next came steel wheels, which required large paddles (called lugs or grousers) to gain traction in the dirt. Rims widened and grew when designers tried to support, or "float," them on the dirt. Some extension rims reached 15 feet from each side. But with no flex, thick steel rims and rigid spokes transmitted every shock. Operators and drivelines suffered each jolt, bump, and slip. By 1907 and 1908, designers discovered that smaller wheels offered better traction and were easier on the tractors. Rumely, Heider, Aultman-Taylor, and others shrunk front steering and rear drive wheels to less-than-human proportions by 1910 and 1911. Engineers stabilized lug length at 4 inches for most wheels and soil types. In California, Samson introduced a "sieve grip" open wheel in 1913 for work on soft sandy soils; a year later, another Californian, manufacturer, Fageol, provided rear wheels that were hubs with long grousers. Further improvements stalled until Oliver Hart-Parr introduced Tip-Toe wheels on its 1930 Row Crop model. These wheels maximized penetration to aid traction. Still, steel wheels had clear limits, and many engineers concluded that crawlers would replace wheels. Crawler tracks, they argued, reduced soil compaction while accommodating more horsepower with less slippage. But that was not what Harvey Firestone wanted to hear.

In the early days of the automobile, pneumatic ("air") tires were the worst part of driving. Long trips required several spares. Tire-makers Firestone and Goodyear made their products stronger and

Originally conceived as a tractor to replace the Fordson, Allis-Chalmers designed and produced the U for the United Tractor and Equipment Company. This group was formed by former Fordson tractor and implement distributors who were stranded in 1929 when Ford transferred production to Ireland.

more reliable; when they perfected self-beading tires, they left behind the awful work of mounting tires on clincher rims. Trucks and airplanes grew in weight and increased their speed, pushing technology even further. Starting in the mid-1920s, brave pioneers tried "air tires" on tractors.

First efforts were mostly for special purposes. By 1925 industrial tractors ran solid rubber tires or high-pressure truck tires in factory environments. In Iowa, an International Harvester distributor and a truck tire dealer put truck tires on Farmalls with mounted corn pickers, thereby cutting harvest time in half. Some orchard and grove operators in Florida tried lower-pressure airplane pneumatics in the late 1920s. Deep grousers on

steel wheels had cut and slashed root systems. But these trials were independent efforts. No manufacturer offered air tires as attachments, let alone regular equipment. Yet.

In the 1930s, Allis-Chalmers had become a fertile hotbed of invention with tillage and planting tools and tractor-mounted or towed gleaners and harvesters. One of the driving forces behind A-C's innovation was Henry Ford's decision to transfer his Fordson production to Ireland. Dozens of implement manufacturers relied on markets created by the Fordson; they were stranded when Ford transferred production overseas. Newly formed Oliver Hart-Parr responded in 1929 with its own tractor, while the others formed the United Tractor and Equipment Company. United approached Allis-Chalmers to build a tractor to replace and improve upon the Fordson. Allis' tractor division general manager Harry Merritt agreed, and chief engineer C. E. Frudden, late of Hart-Parr, designed the U (with rumored help from Charles Parr himself) to work in both agricultural and industrial markets.

The U was a good, steady tractor. But it closely followed the Fordson, which by then was an old, outdated design (something United Company–member Harry

A basic, simple tractor, the Model U returned to Allis-Chalmers' catalog when United disbanded in 1931. The 1929 and 1930 United used a four-cylinder Continental 4.25x5.0-inch engine, while the 1931 A-C U used a Waukesha. In late 1932, Allis-Chalmers installed its own UM 4.375x5.0 engine.

The most significant contribution of the Model U was its introduction of pneumatic rubber (or "air tires") to farmers. A-C's general manager Harry Merritt heard of Iowa implement dealers mounting truck tires on Farmalls during the corn harvest. He approached Harvey Firestone, who wanted to see air tires on everything that moved.

Ferguson frequently noted). However, hearing about the Iowa Farmalls on truck tires, Merritt and Frudden contacted tire manufacturer (and gentleman farmer) Harvey Firestone in Akron, Ohio. Firestone wanted balloon tires on all vehicles. He believed the quiet, smooth ride would help farmers by decreasing slip, absorbing shock, and decreasing fatigue. He and Merritt turned A-C's old Model U design into an innovation. After extensive private sessions, A-C first publicly tested the Firestone-shod U on Albert Schroeder's farm in nearby Waukesha, Wisconsin. The air tires increased efficiency, rolled more easily over hard and soft soil, and their flexibility was easier on operators' backs, allowing them to work longer days. Allis and Firestone moved quickly to offer the tires to other customers. Allis also followed up with additional lightweight tractor designs, including the WC and B, to utilize the new tires.

But offering the new tires for sale wasn't enough. Many farmers claimed the new tires (and added weight) would compact the soil. Some feared that rubber dust from the tires would poison the soil or their crops. Skeptics knew the new tires wouldn't hold up to field duty. Many competing manufacturers began a campaign against the rubber tires.

Allis had two things going for it to silence the naysayers. The first was that everyone had done their homework. The new tires worked well and had long lives. Allis began working with other tire manufacturers on tire design, especially tread patterns and profiles. The second thing came straight from Harry Merritt's fertile mind.

Merritt hired auto-racing legend Barney Oldfield and outfitted several Model U tractors with higher-speed gears and rubber tires. Wilder speed would be more accurate. Oldfield, Ab Jenkins, and several other racers barnstormed the country, delighting fans at local fairs by driving Merritt's Persian orange tractors at speeds beyond what most automobiles could reach. Oldfield's original auto-racing career began on flat dirt tracks. That experience prepared him for tractors with high centers of gravity. Oldfield's contract with Merritt guaranteed he always won but he also set a "closed-track" record of more than 62 miles per hour.

The sales campaign helped to end skepticism about the durability, the traction, and the ride on rubber tires. Resistance decreased rapidly, although some farmers continued for decades to believe that farming was hard and noble work, and anything that made it easier was a sacrilege.

Albert Schroeder, a dairy farmer near Waukesha, Wisconsin, was the test farmer for Allis-Chalmers' new rubber-tired Model U. He was pleased, but rubber skeptics were convinced only after seeing racing greats Ab Jenkins and Barney Oldfield use rubber-tired Model U tractors as they raced against all comers at local county fairs.

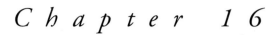

1935 Oliver Hart-Parr Row Crop 70

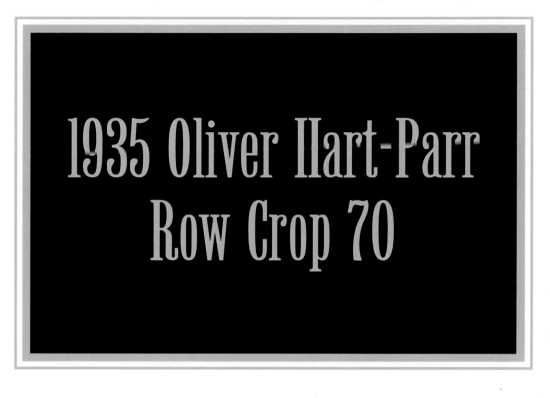

E arly in 1935, the Oliver 70 set a direction that all farm tractors followed for the next 20 years. The tractor combined a sleek exterior with farming's first engine designed to use the new 70-octane gasoline. Introduced three years after the darkest days of the Depression, Oliver's timing was perfect. President Franklin Roosevelt's New Deal restored the spending power of Americans. The cash flow excited the public's interest in styling and new technology. The Oliver 70 provided both. Chief engineer Herman Altgelt and his staff improved the power output of Oliver's four-cylinder engines by increasing their compression. The complete package generated several copies of both engine design and exterior styling through the next decade as Deere, Minneapolis-Moline, Case, IHC, and even Ford sought to catch up with Oliver and then fought to regain their former customers.

The Oliver 70's styling was masterful. Other tractor makers had paid attention to the machine's appearance but none had yet put together a full package. Some, like Huber's Modern Farmer tractor, and Massey-Harris' Model 25s, merely cast their name into a more appealingly shaped radiator. Several went further, already aware of the benefits of industrial design. Caterpillar had introduced ergonomic seats in 1931, designed so that the operator could more comfortably use Cat's or LeTourneau's rear-mounted cable control units for front-mounted blades or towed-behind scrapers. Fate-Root-Heath, for its 1933 Plymouth Model 10-20, had devised an attractive-looking radiator and grille shell that covered the actual radiator upper tank, but they stopped there. The 10-20's rear end looked like the old, traditional rolling pile of iron. The International Harvester Corporation

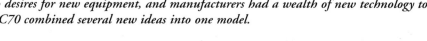

By the time the economy recovered from the disastrous Depression era of 1929 to 1932, farmers had pent-up desires for new equipment, and manufacturers had a wealth of new technology to offer. The RC70 combined several new ideas into one model.

had created a stylish package in its big Waite tractor a decade earlier; this prototype, however, was never produced in any number. Few outside the company were even aware that the prototype existed.

What Oliver did right was not only the front end but also the operator's platform and the tractor back end. Most important, Oliver put the whole, integrated design into production.

The petroleum industry changed in the 1930s as well. Higher-performance automotive engines encouraged tractor manufacturers to consider the power improvements available with more potent fuel. In the early 1930s, gasoline provided little more than a 45- to 55-octane rating. Petroleum distillers began adding lead, which allowed higher output yet cooler running temperatures; producers collectively changed their processes and their marketing efforts. Gasoline universally reached 70-octane by the middle of the decade. The refiners vigorously promoted the product, liberally funding agricultural engineering school research programs to prove their claims.

The model designation "70" represented the gasoline octane rating that Oliver had in mind in developing this new engine. Higher octane fuels provided greater performance without increasing engine displacement. On gasoline, the engine developed 26.6 horsepower compared with 24.8 on distillate fuel.

Chief engineer Herman Altgelt supervised the exterior design of the tractor sheet metal. The streamline age had begun, and automobiles, trucks, trains, and airplanes started to appear with curved lines that seemed shaped by the wind. Oliver's designers were not first, but they were the most daring.

Oliver's Herman Altgelt was the first to design a tractor engine to take advantage of the change. While kerosene and distillate fuels had not changed (except for their steadily rising prices), gasoline offered higher-octane ratings without price increases. Higher octane provided more power and power was what farmers sought. What's more, gasoline had none of the problems of oil dilution and poor compression caused by the other fuels.

In another 10 years, both kerosene and distillate fuels virtually disappeared from production, knocked from the positions of dominance they'd held since the late 1900s. The gasoline makers used the improved performance potential of their product to defeat their competitors while hooking farmers with its results. Producers even decided to hold prices at the levels of the lower-octane fuels, giving the new blends an even greater advantage over the lower-rated gasoline.

The Oliver Hart-Parr 70 had two other features—its configuration and its rear axles—that dated from the time before Oliver and Hart-Parr joined forces to form the new Oliver Corporation. Oliver Plow Company had begun to design a row-crop tractor in reaction to Henry Ford's relocation of Fordson production from Dearborn, Michigan, to Cork, Ireland. Besides greatly decreasing availability, Ford's

relocation forced a price increase on the ubiquitous Fordson that nearly eliminated sales from U.S. markets. Oliver knew that Ford's tractor engineers had begun to develop row-crop tractors. But the move to Ireland (a nation without much row-crop agriculture), as well as other business matters, delayed Ford's introduction for another decade. Since Oliver's main market for its farm implement divisions had been Fordson tractors and owners, the new situation left Oliver in a tight squeeze. Designing and producing its own row-crop model, as well as dedicated implements, guaranteed that Oliver and its implement divisions had a future.

Altgelt and his group designed the Row Crop 70 without using drop-axle housings, which International's Philo Danly, David Baker, and Bert Benjamin had used to improve crop clearance on their Farmall. Oliver's splined, long axles meant that infinitely variable wheel spacings were possible, with a wide range of widths available to the farmer, just by moving the wheels in or out along the axles.

Even Oliver's wheels were novel. Oliver pioneered the "tip toe" wheel. These used common skeleton wheels but with deep, solid lugs at the rim. This combination provided excellent ground penetration and traction (for certain, though not all, soil types). Several competitors copied Oliver's Tip-Toe wheels, and farmers and many engineers generally considered these the ultimate—and final—development of steel wheels.

Progress is often denoted by a single notch on the workbench. With its striking appearance and its high-tech engine, Oliver Hart-Parr moved the mechanical farming benchmark forward considerably. But progress sometimes needs to be considered as a yardstick that pushes one end and pulls the other. Allis-Chalmers had recently moved the notch with rubber tires in an effort to improve traction and decrease compaction. With its Tip-Toe wheels, Oliver proved progress was possible even at the tail end of development.

Another Oliver Hart-Parr/Herman Altgelt concern was soil compaction, and Altgelt's staff created a remarkable steel wheel with an impossibly narrow band supporting stubby pointed grousers. Oliver named these "Tip-Toes," and this tractor sports the rare dual rear wheels.

Oliver also set the standard for styling with this new machine. No one really knows who penned the lines of the attractive Row Crop series that first appeared in 1935, but Oliver's chief engineer, Herman Altgelt, not only supervised the sleek appearance but also the logical reorganization of the operator platform.

Minneapolis-Moline 1937 Model U-DLX Comfortractor

F arming is noble work. It requires long hours in changing conditions. The day may begin under a warming sun and end in numbing darkness. Wind, blowing dust, and straw slap faces. Droning engines dull the senses and deaden hearing. Even on rubber tires, the ride pounds the body. Deep fatigue induces illness, forcing downtime on farmers, or it clouds judgment, sometimes causing poor decisions or accidents. Reducing fatigue increases productivity. It's that simple.

A century ago, steam traction engine makers set canopies over their engines to deflect the rain since few farmers had large sheds. Some even extended covers back to shelter operators on sunny days. A decade later, canopies had become crude cab-and-cover combinations. In the early 1900s, a very few makers who produced the large prairie sod-busters—such as Hart-Parr's 60-100, IHC's Friction Drives (with an optional cab), the Waite 20-horsepower friction drive, Pioneer Tractor's Model Thirty, and Savage Harvester's 20-35—experimented with glass in cabs. Many others introduced canvas weather curtains.

As tractors got smaller, cabs and canopies became less prevalent. The Bull, Fordson, and other small tractors whose appeal to farmers was their low cost, eliminated canopies and cabs or made them high-price add-ons. Farmers who walked behind horses and oxen without protection didn't need or expect it now.

In the early 1930s rubber air-pressurized tires appeared. Tractor speeds rose as farmers learned their new machines could haul wagons to town. In demonstrating rubber tires, tractor racer Barney

It was controversial and it was expensive. So it was unpopular. Farmers balked at its price and felt self-conscious about the luxury the U-DLX suggested. Minneapolis-Moline's designer, Nels Erickson, created the enclosed cab tractor about 50 years before farmers were ready.

standard features including roll-up side windows, cigar lighter, heater, windshield wipers, radio, roof spotlight, and a bifold swing-open rear door. M-M created the name "Comfortractor" for this new machine.

Minneapolis-Moline didn't stop there. Reasoning that its U-DLX had features rivaling many motor trucks that were currently available, Nels Erickson devised an air-brake system intended to work on large trailers loaded with grain, produce, or livestock. He tested and patented the system, although no one can say for sure if M-M produced more than a few prototypes.

The market looked at the U-DLX and then shuffled its feet. Noble farmers are a hard audience. M-M aimed the Comfortractor squarely at a market captivated by row-crop tractors. Critics told farmers they couldn't shift cultivator gangs or adjust plows inside the closed cab. The Comfortractor's price also hurt its sales. The Comfortractor retailed for $2,155, when the average American farmer's annual net income was one-third of that—a figure with which he could still buy a Sears, Roebuck and Co. kit house.

Roosevelt's New Deal had worked so well that, to control the kind of inflation that offered $2,000 luxury tractors, he cut federal spending 10 percent in 1937 and 1938. (This triggered the onset of Depression II, an eco-

The U-DLX gave farmers roll-up windows, a weather-proof cab with a heater and windshield wipers, and a radio. Designer Nels Erickson's idea was to provide the farmers a tractor for fieldwork during the week and an automobile to go to town in on weekends. A flip-up buddy seat offered cozy accommodations for a family.

Oldfield ran faster than 60 miles per hour, but neither farmers nor manufacturers believed this was necessary for regular production. Still, no one knew how fast was fast enough. Minneapolis-Moline, like others, used farmer surveys to try ideas and to track trends. Minneapolis-Moline was startled by the following survey suggestion: "It would be great if one could only have a cab on a tractor—at a price one could afford—at no sacrifice to cultivation."

Ready to introduce its stylish Vision-Lined U-series of tractors, Minnie-Mo returned engineer Nels Erickson to his drawing boards. Rubber tires allowed higher speeds; M-M added a fifth gear good for 40 miles per hour on a tractor it would create with a cab. High speeds required special bearings, and a different transmission and clutch. Now farmers had a tractor that kept pace with contemporary automobiles going into town (of course, cars carried more passengers).

M-M also added a buddy seat, an electric starter, stop lights, and bodywork that gave Erickson the chance to add fenders and chrome bumpers to the Vision Line. In addition, Erickson devised a removable right front fender to provide access to the belt pulley.

But Minneapolis-Moline hedged its bets. As it created this deluxe model, M-M worried the cab might be too much. After all, this came on the heels of the Great Depression. The economy was improving, but . . . So Erickson also designed a "Deluxe Tractor Open Cab." It took some doing, but Erickson devised a method of adding the cab if the buyer chose to do so. The cab, factory installed or mounted later by the dealer, offered

Rubber tires on tractors allowed them to work and to travel at higher speeds. Erickson added a fifth gear and stronger engine and transmission bearings to Minneapolis-Moline's Model U, allowing farmers a 40-mile-per-hour top speed. Electric starting also provided a generator for headlights and a roof-mounted spotlight.

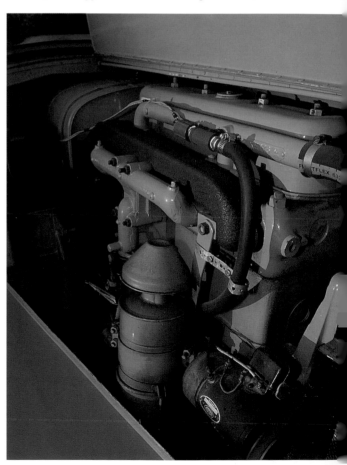

nomic collapse in 1938 and 1939 that required a new World War to reverse.) Minnie-Mo's problem was clear. The Comfortractor may have been what some farmers asked for, but it certainly appeared at the wrong time. M-M built something like 125 with cabs and perhaps only another 75 without. M-M then offered cabs on its Model R, a cultivating tractor, but these too were not widely popular even though gang adjustments were possible from inside. M-M stuck cabs on a few of their military tractors, but the government wouldn't pay for the additional expense. Soldiering is a noble profession, as well.

The Comfortractor made the industry think about cabs. M-M distributors towed binders to customers and demonstrated the implements with their U-DLXs in the early 1940s. As early as the 1950s, when tractors grew in power and price, cabs began to reappear. Many features of the U-DLX showed up, including cigar lighters and additional exterior lighting.

Other features reached markets in the 1990s. Harvesters offer a buddy seat and many tractor makers have one available. Air conditioning replaced roll-up windows. The simple radio is now a cassette player/CD changer/cellular phone. Deere & Co., Case-New Holland, and several European makers are running prototypes with 40-miles-per-hour top speeds and air brakes.

Farming is still a noble profession, and days now often begin and end in the dark. But farmers and manufacturers alike recognize that comfort is no longer a crime but a benefit.

Nels Erickson had created the "Vision Line" series of tractors, M-M's styled, streamlined machines. But Erickson went the furthest to emulate the sleek automobiles and trucks of the period. Another of his innovations was the removable right front fender, which provided access to a belt pulley.

The folding rear door gave farmers and families access to the U-DLX interior. But while the nation's economy had improved, not everyone had reached the comfort zone yet. Minneapolis-Moline offered an open version of the U, which had fenders and electric lights. Buyers could order the cab from dealers later. Few did so.

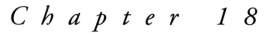

Allis-Chalmers 1937 Model B

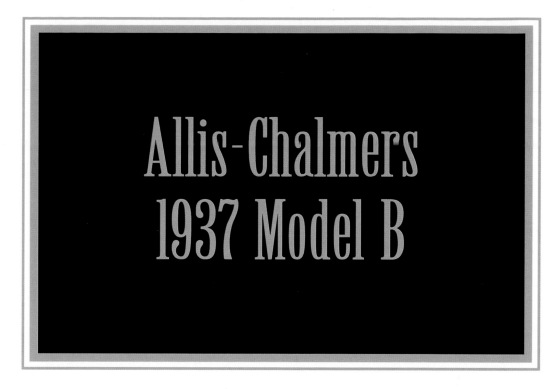

By the early 1930s, small, cheap machines left a bad taste in everyone's mouth. The number of tractors of all sizes on farms in the United States had jumped from some 246,000 in 1920 to more than 920,000 in 1930. Most of this increase came at the lower price end of the market. Created by D. M. Hartsough, the Little and Big Bulls arrived first, with their dubious layouts and mechanical eccentricities, not to mention their inherent inability to plow in a straight line. Henry Ford's Fordson had been an undisputed sales success, but farmers' ability to flip it over and its reputation for being nearly impossible to start in winter had damaged its credibility. Ford left it too long on the market without improvements, while the rest of the marketplace plowed ahead. Once Ford exiled its manufacture to Ireland, farmers saw Fordsons as damaged goods on the used-tractor market, worth nearly nothing when they traded for new row-crops and more modern, reliable, standard tractors.

The Fordson had opened new markets, the small farms targeted by Ford. With Fordson now classified as a pricey import, these farmers went begging for new tractors. International's solution for the one- or two-horse farms came in 1932 when it introduced the 12 series of tractors. The line included the F-12, a two-row row-crop tractor; the I-12, a tidy industrial tractor; the O-12, an orchard version; and the W-12, a compact standard tractor. These machines all featured a new semi-unitized frame-rail-and-transmission-case construction that reduced weight and kept the design compact and efficient. The 12 series sold very well despite nagging mechanical problems. Their main drawback was that they were still too big. The 12 series tractors were a two-row size when

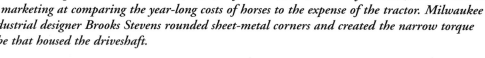

Allis-Chalmers priced the Model B at $495 (only about $5,825 in today's dollars), and it aimed its marketing at comparing the year-long costs of horses to the expense of the tractor. Milwaukee industrial designer Brooks Stevens rounded sheet-metal corners and created the narrow torque tube that housed the driveshaft.

Allis-Chalmer's Model B tractor was designed, as it had done with the WC model, to use rubber tires from the start. Its wide padded seat allowed farmers to easily shift their view from one side of the tractor to the other. This gave farmers as much visibility as they'd had cultivating with horses.

many farmers had one-row farms. Millions of farms still found it too expensive to buy a tractor.

The industry's first tractor tailored to the single-row farmer would come from Allis-Chalmers, a company with experience in designing affordable, efficient tractors. Allis demonstrated their savvy for new materials with its two-row model, the WC. The WC was designed for rubber tires, which allowed the tractor to be lighter without sacrificing durability. The WC came out in 1934, a year after Franklin Roosevelt's New Deal economic repairs began to have an impact. The Agricultural Adjustment Act, meant to increase demand and prices by reducing supply, compensated farmers for limiting production. The Emergency Farm Mortgage Act and the Farm Credit Act of 1933 expanded the federal land banks, making available desperately needed funds.

The farmers had access to cash, but the industry's two-row tractors did not meet the needs of the one-row farmers. These small farms, although feeling at last included in the nation's financial uplift, still felt excluded by tractor makers. What they needed, what even many large operations could use, was a one-row tractor. (In 1932, incredibly, America's farmland had maxed out. All that could be cultivated, something like 371 million acres, was in use. The only land remaining was what became available once farmers no longer fed draft animals.) One-row farming was the foundation of most small operations, particularly with truck farmers, who used transplanters. These required two people for each row, plus a driver. During the Depression, truck farmers had difficulty finding—and paying—labor willing to work in agriculture. Hungry hands flooded the cities hoping for industrial work with regular hours. For the small farmer, getting by with two fewer people was an economic necessity.

Allis solved this problem with the one-row Model B. In doing so, A-C created not only a very popular tractor, but also introduced a new frame design. This innovation was the torque tube, the long cast-iron cylinder extending from the clutch to the transmission. The torque tube was essentially a spacer, making the tractor longer, which improved stability. But it also reduced the angle at which the operator had to look down to see cultivators. The torque tube made the tractor thinner, mainly through this same area where operators watched the crops. Farmers peered around the slender tube rather than around a wide channel-iron frame, fuel tank, engine hood, or other obstruction on the bigger two-row models. The torque tube proved to be necessary to the competition as well, and Allis harvested patent fees from several other companies. The torque tube, coupled to a compact transmission under the operator, and a small Waukesha engine (fitted only in the first 97 prototypes; in later-production models A-C used their own powerplant), produced a wasp-waist-shaped tractor that may have inspired the name "B." This machine was very cheap to produce. In assembly, workers built it from both ends of the tube in a very space-efficient manner.

Besides the torque tube, another new feature that proved difficult for competitors to avoid patent infringement was the Model B's narrow fuel tank support. This was a thin, U-shaped piece of sheet metal that, again, stayed clear of the operator's line of vision to the single crop row slipping between the wheels below.

To complete the package, Allis-Chalmers produced a set of matched implements, tools, and other equipment for its nearly 13-drawbar horsepower Model B, which could handle most of the jobs on an average farm. The Model B's total price, including the small 4-foot-cut combine, came to slightly less than $1,000 (about $12,000 adjusted to inflation today)—an investment that completely mechanized a two- or three-horse farm. The B provided small farm owners with a powerful incentive to go tractor farming in the late 1930s. The B also offered clear inspiration to competitors such as Ford, Deere, Massey, and International Harvester.

Previous page, upper right: Allis-Chalmers conceived this tractor to appeal to small farm operators who had been frightened away from mechanization by its costs and limitations. As Ford had done with the Fordson, Allis-Chalmers set its sights on farmers who still used only horses.

This Waukesha inline four-cylinder engine measured 3x4 inches and developed about two-thirds of the power of Allis-Chalmer's larger WC two-plow-rated models. Allis-Chalmers used this engine only in the first 96 Model Bs produced. Starting in 1938, the company provided its own new 3.25x3.5-inch engine, which developed 12.9 drawbar and 15.7 belt pulley horsepower at 1,400 rpm.

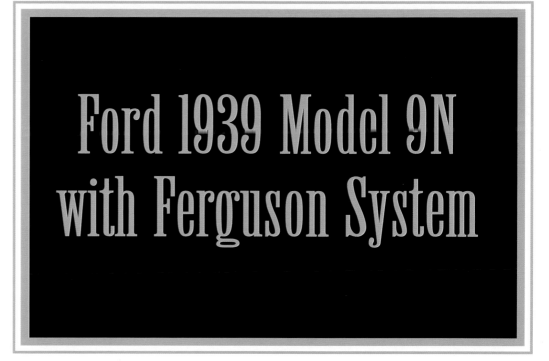

Ford 1939 Model 9N with Ferguson System

Henry Ford transferred Fordson production to Ireland in 1928, fulfilling a long-time promise to bring jobs to his homeland. This move also kept him in tractor production. Ford loved tractors. He liked automobiles and trucks for the power, influence, and financial resources they gave him. These resources provided him the independence he needed to build his tractors.

However, moving tractor production to Europe left Ford's dealers high and dry when they learned Cork would export no more than 1,500 Fordsons a month. Oliver Chilled Plow, long a primary supplier, merged in 1929 with Hart-Parr who, soon after, introduced their Row Crop tractor as an Oliver Hart-Parr. But 32 other dealers and suppliers affected by the Fordson move formed United Tractor & Equipment Corporation. United approached Allis-Chalmers to build a tractor similar to the Fordson in function but improved and more powerful. Allis created the three-plow "United" and everyone was content.

Everyone was content except Ford, who missed tractors. He was preoccupied with two other matters. One distraction was the auto industry's first V-8 engine. Following five years of development, Ford introduced the V-8 on March 31, 1932, installed in Model A body cars. Ten months later, he introduced a sleek new 1933 Model B body to surround the engine. The project was nearly all consuming.

The other matter took place in a federal court in New York. In mid-July 1931, after 14 years of investigation, prosecution, and appeals, the government dismissed charges of fraud against the

Henry Ford didn't have an easy time getting from his solid but unsophisticated Fordson to his next production tractor. His engineers tried many ideas, as they had 35 years earlier, and as with the Fordson, it took outside inspiration to nudge Ford in the right direction.

wheels, to the Eros tractor and resisted the rearing-up motion. After World War II they improved the plow, lightening and strengthening each element, making it simpler with each version. Ferguson and Sands incorporated automatic, hydraulically operated draft control to maintain plow depth no matter what the tractor did. Ferguson hoped to interest Ford—or any manufacturer—in his ideas and, in post-Depression 1933, he spent all his money to build one prototype Ferguson tractor that he painted black. Soon English gear-maker David Brown agreed to produce the Ferguson and its plow. But Ferguson still wanted U.S. distribution and he really wanted Ford.

After five days of plowing at Ford's Fairlane Farm in Dearborn, Ford called for a table and chairs for himself and Ferguson. They came to terms, stood up, shook hands on a "gentlemen's agreement," posed for pictures, and launched a whirlwind of activity. Overnight, Ferguson was wealthy and influential and became a pain to Ford engineer Howard Simpson, who disassembled Ferguson's tractor to make it something Ford could produce. Harold Brock joined the project when Simpson left Ford. Ford brought in an Allis-Chalmers Model B and made it clear that his new tractor should incorporate the best ideas and technology of the B and the Ferguson. Designated the 9N, "9" being its year of introduction and "N" being Ford's internal

Ford carried over the unitized-frame construction of his Fordson into the new 9N model, so named because 1939 was the year of introduction and "N" was Ford Motor Company's internal designation for tractor products.

Ford Tractor Company of Minneapolis, Minnesota. This fly-by-night operation, out of business since the investigation began, had usurped Ford's name, forcing him to brand his own machine the Fordson. Now, with no pretenders claiming his name, Ford's name was his own to put on a new tractor.

Within days Ford set engineers Gene Farkas, Howard Simpson, and Karl Schultz to work designing a new machine, then another, and another. Ford's motto became, "Let's start it up and see why it doesn't work." Schultz and Simpson created row-crop tricycles with V-8s mounted front-to-rear, one-wheel-drive transverse-V-8 variations, ultra-lightweight unit-frame prototypes with inline truck engines, and tiny twin-cylinder air-cooled versions. Some wouldn't steer; some broke in two. Ford encouraged them to keep trying.

Then, over a few days in November 1938, George and Eber Sherman, two New York businessmen who handled the Irish Fordson import business to the United States, introduced Ford to another Irish import, Harry Ferguson. Ferguson had sold tractors by demonstrating them. During World War II, the Irish government hired Ferguson to teach farmers to use Fordsons and other machines, including E. G. Staude's Eros Model T conversion. Ferguson's partner, Willie Sands, created a two-bottom plow that attached, without any

The 9N was an incredibly simple machine, and Ford's engineers drew upon both Harry Ferguson's remarkable tractor and prototypes of Allis-Chalmers' Model B tractor that Ford and others had heard about. The 9N weighed 2,340 pounds, just 240 pounds more than the Allis B.

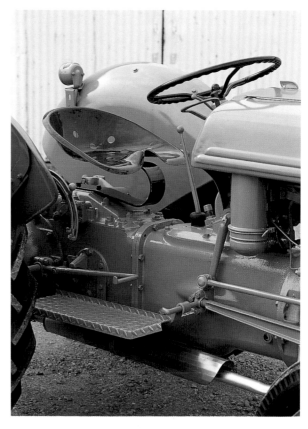

code for tractors, Brock redesigned the transmission and entire hydraulic system and then replaced Ferguson's engine with one bank from Ford's new Mercury 95-horsepower V-8. Styling chief Eugene Gregoire and Ed Scott, Ford's designer at the huge Rouge Plant (where the tractor would be built), created the simple, stylish sheet metal and grille. Production began slowly on June 5, 1939, and only 6,849 were built by year-end. But in true Ford fashion, the Rouge Plant released 90,000 tractors in 1940.

Ford again declined to produce implements, ironic since the tractor's greatest improvement was Ferguson's and Sands' three-point hitch. Its geometry allowed the tractor to work like machines much larger and heavier, and Brock's revised hydraulics made the system a delight. But the marriage made on Fairlane Farm and consummated in Ford's Rouge Plant was fiery and short-lived, ending in court.

Ford and Ferguson's court battle saw the two companies split, creating two separate tractor lines. Ford 9N Tractor badges acknowledged Ferguson's system. The system remained in Ford's 2N models, but the badge disappeared. By Ford's 1948 8N model change, Ferguson was producing a 9N clone, his TE-20, for Tractor, Europe, 20 horsepower, or TO-20 for overseas export.

Ferguson ultimately demanded $342 million in damages and royalties for unauthorized use of his system on tens of thousands of 2N and 8N tractors. Four years later, Ford wrote Ferguson a check for $9.25 million for royalties alone. Ferguson continued independently until Canada's Massey-Harris in 1953 proposed a merger, becoming Massey-Harris-Ferguson and in 1958 just Massey-Ferguson.

Back in the 1930s, Ford had told Harold Brock to study Allis' Model B but not copy it, to size his new tractor properly for row-crop work. But it should not look—or work—like anyone else's. Yet Ferguson's hitch and Brock's hydraulics sent the others back to the drawing boards, trying to provide for their customers without infringing on Ford's patents.

After Ford's death, the company copied others, producing row-crop tricycles into the 1980s. But the instability of narrow fronts led everyone back to Ford's basic configuration. Nearly every manufacturer's tractor now resembles the machine that wouldn't copy the others: Ford's simple 9N.

Harry Ferguson and his mechanical partner, Willie Sands, created the most significant development up to that time: the three-point hitch and hydraulic draft control. The system carried dedicated implements rather than dragging them behind on the optional drawbar. Ferguson's and Sands' system forced down the nose of the tractor under hard pulling.

Size was important to Ford. He still found other tractor makers to be no competition, and he went after farmers still using horses. The little 9N was only 115 inches long, 64 inches wide, and 52 inches tall. Standard rubber was 4.00x19 front and 8.00x32 rear tires.

Chapter 20

International Harvester 1939 Farmall A

The Farmall A was IHC's direct—some might say frantic—response to the Allis-Chalmers Model B. In some ways, it was a direct copy of the B. (A-C later claimed exactly that and threatened to take International Harvester to court.) The small Farmall took advantage of features already introduced on IHC's other models. IHC engineers in Chicago produced something that observers called "flamboyant design." This engine offset was, and still is, copied.

When the Allis B appeared for field-testing in 1935, International Harvester's field organization spotted it almost immediately. IHC's response to this sighting swept throughout company. Their sales department alerted its vast dealer and branch house network, and people quickly located other Bs in the field. Soon, IHC's Gas Power Engineering Department was receiving field development reports about the B shortly after engineers at A-C's Milwaukee headquarters did. In fact, because so many people were watching and reporting on the B, Chicago probably had some information before Milwaukee did.

IHC immediately began developing a tractor to compete with the B. Enthusiasm for the project was widespread. At least one engineer had wanted to build the Farmall F-12 smaller than it was. Russell Action now pointed out that Allis-Chalmers had proven his point. The new project proceeded quickly, perhaps too quickly. Even though IHC had seen the competition, even though its board of directors agreed on the need to compete, there was fear in Chicago.

Farmall's Model A also was inspired by Allis-Chalmers' Model B. While it didn't have Harry Ferguson's and Willie Sands' innovative three-point hitch system, IHC took the Allis-Chalmers tractor idea a step further as a machine designed for cultivating on small farms.

International used its own inline four-cylinder 3 x 4-inch engine for the A. It produced a maximum of 15.2 drawbar and 16.5 PTO horsepower at its rated 1,400 rpm. Ballasted down for its Nebraska tests, it tugged a maximum of 2,360 pounds using distillate fuels.

International Harvester didn't know what Allis-Chalmers intended to claim as original, or what were "improvements on the existing art" for its patent on the B. Chicago needed to avoid infringements as it had recently lost a decades-long squabble with Caterpillar. But how could it rush into production its answer to the B without asking some questions? Incredibly, IHC asked Allis what its position was on the B patents. Not surprisingly, Milwaukee was uncommunicative. The long-standing, close relationship between the two manufacturers surely played a role in falsely reassuring IHC.

One fundamental change that IHC made to avoid the Allis patents was to alter the layout and sight lines of its tractor. The B's narrow-waisted torque-tube construction forced operators to look around the tube. IHC created an offset tractor. The experimental department shifted the powertrain about 8 inches to the left of the centerline on the tractor. This gave operators an unimpeded view of the cultivators (or any other implement) working in front or below them. Tractor engineering fitted a wide, offset front axle. This allowed a single row to pass between the two front tires. IHC named their design the "Cultivision."

Ultimately, the Cultivision idea wasn't enough to avoid infringing on the Allis patents. After the Farmall A made its appearance in 1939 to great success, Allis informed IHC that it was, after all, in violation of its just-issued patents. IHC fought, and eventually settled

At least one engineer within International's Gas Power Engineering department had argued with the executive committee that the company's F-12 was still too large for the small farms served by horses. Allis-Chalmer's Model B and then Ford's 9N were designed from the same beliefs.

out of court. IHC had to pay Allis-Chalmers $35,000.

Cultivision's offset layout proved both popular and long-lived. It took a big piece of the sales that Allis had with its Model B, but IHC didn't stop with its A. The Farmall B soon followed, featuring narrow fronts and a wider rear axle on the left side to accommodate two-row cultivation. IHC then produced the Farmall BN, a narrow-tread version of its B.

In 1947, IHC revamped the tractors. It eliminated the Model B and added live hydraulics onto the A, which it renamed the Super A. Other (slight) modifications followed, as Tractor Engineering enlarged engines, improved hydraulics, and strengthened hitches. IHC also restyled the tractor sheet metal. The Super A briefly became the Super A-1. Then it was called the 100, the 130, and last, the 140, which finally straggled out of production in 1980. IHC had stretched more than 40 years out of that initial panic attack. However, the story took another turn long before 1980.

In the mid-1940s, IHC sought to design a smaller tractor, one specifically meant for the compact farms in the South, where it would replace one mule or horse. What Tractor Engineering eventually did was create a two thirds-scale model of the Farmall Super A. Known internally for some time as the Farmall X, Sales advocated using a name to designate that it was something new. After examining and eliminating hundreds of possibilities, IHC settled on the Cub.

The Cub used the Cultivision system developed for the Farmall A. It, too, was a long-lived success and the Cub, Cub Lo-Boy, and a few other variations lasted in production until 1980. But the story didn't finish there, either.

The Cub, essentially a scaled-down farm tractor, was well designed and over built. It possessed great durability and strength. In the late 1950s, IHC took a serious look at the lawn tractor market and concluded that even its Cub was too large. IHC engineers adopted the Cub rear axle and transmission assembly, then mounted a Kohler air-cooled engine in front of it and fitted smaller tires all around it. They named this machine the Cub Cadet. Its strong farm tractor driveline ensured success for the Cadets that followed. The Cub Cadet remained in production into the mid-1990s, 60 years after IHC first feared it had a big problem on its hands in the shape of a little orange tractor.

International Harvester was very concerned about patent infringement on Allis' Model B with its torque-tube narrow waist that allowed excellent ground visibility. So International shifted the powertrain about 8 inches to the left of the tractor centerline and offered only a wide front axle that was similarly offset. They called the design "Cultivision."

The offset Cultivision design allowed operators an even better view of the work going on between the wheels than Allis owners, who had to look to the left or right around the torque tube. International quickly devised many one-row implements, including this grader blade, to take advantage of the excellent visibility.

Minneapolis-Moline 1941 Model U Liquefied Petroleum Gas

When Dr. William Snelling accidentally discovered the stuff, he nicknamed it "greasy air," "air" because it was colorless and odorless, and "greasy" because it would burn. He could think of no possible use for it.

In the early 1920s, motor trucks and automobiles were so numerous and consuming so much gasoline that the petroleum industry got caught short. In 1925 the world suffered a gas shortage. Drillers and refiners responded with new technology. Part of this new technology included processing natural gasolines under much higher pressure, and revising the mixture of naphtha and other substances to make the auto fuel. Higher pressure liquefied some of the by-products. This allowed refiners to begin bottling propane and butane, as a liquid, in containers, rather than just releasing it into the air as an unwanted by-product from the lower-pressure processes. Phillips Petroleum and Union Carbide & Carbon moved in on this new field first. Phillips built an enormous plant at Borger, Texas, specifically to manufacture liquid propane, providing bottled gas for cooking and heating to millions of rural farmers in areas not served by natural gas lines. During 1922, Phillips barely produced 223,000 gallons of propane. Until 1929, a year in which they marketed almost 10 million gallons, Phillips had the business to itself. By the time the stock market crashed, seven other large gasoline manufacturers had begun bottling LPG.

The Depression moved slowly across the country. In 1933 and 1934, farmers began to believe life might improve. To a market hungry for signs of better times, Oliver introduced a sharp new tractor in 1935, styled like expensive automobiles and running on an automotive fuel: 70-octane

LPG provided tractor manufacturers with several benefits. First, the product was cheaper than gasoline—by as much as two-thirds less expensive. Second, because it required a higher compression ratio to combust, the fuel provided higher horsepower output.

accepted loose fittings, grease packing, and rubber compounds to seal tanks and valves, but this vapor easily escaped. Once Phillips resolved these problems, propane demand exploded to 462 million gallons in 1941. Although railcars customarily moved huge tanks, Phillips and Shell began delivering the gas in propane-powered service trucks, showing that the fuel could power vehicles as well.

These "greasy air" fuels were cheap to produce and refiners sold them for less than complicated high-octane gasoline. Butane and propane sold for 4 to 5 cents per gallon; gasoline was 18 cents. As early as 1928, engineers worked on carburetors for LPG. By 1929, George Hofzapel of California had perfected pressure regulators and carburetors.

Through the early 1930s, hundreds of entrepreneurs were outfitting tractors with $150-to-$250 kits. These kits helped farmers shave cylinder heads and substitute high-altitude pistons to increase engine compression to handle the 93-octane-rated butane or 112-octane-rated propane.

One great risk of these bottled gases was their air-like invisibility. State governments feared injuries (in its compressed liquid state, bottled gas was extremely cold; contact with it froze skin instantly) or deaths from farmers inadvertently inhaling it. A Phillips chemical engineer, Emerson Thomas, began odorizing their

Above: Its standard 30-gallon LPG tank was handsomely designed into the hoodline of Minneapolis-Moline's Vision-Lined tractors, an advantage that the company had by designing the tractor to use the cheap fuel. Outside manufacturers and converters just shoe-horned the tanks wherever they could fit them.

gasoline. Oliver's engine required higher compression to use this fuel but in return, it produced higher horsepower. It needed antiknock agents, such as tetraethyl lead, to work right, so cheaper 44- to 55-octane natural gasoline was not usable. As the economy strengthened, the demand for high-octane gasoline rose as well. As styled tractors and sleek autos filled the farm journals, farmers became modern at home too. They could update wood stoves with those using bottled gas. While the world consumed 10 million gallons of propane and butane in 1929, usage increased to 56 million gallons in 1934.

At first, transporting the gas in tanks was risky. LPG not only operated under high pressure but it also had solvent qualities. The petroleum industry had

product long before the U.S. Bureau of Mines adopted Ethyl Mercaptan, known as the "smelliest substance on earth." The industry set the mix at 1 pound per 10,000 gallons, and it's still in use today.

Tractor manufacturers watched this phenomenon. In central California alone, an industrious group had converted 20,000 tractors to butane or propane fuel during the 1930s. Minneapolis-Moline was among the first to seriously consider it.

"Fuel economy is the most important factor in considering the operating data of any engine," M-M engineer Marvin Samuelson said to the Society of Automotive Engineers in 1951, 10 years after M-M followed through on its LPG hunch. "In as much as fuel consumption represents out-of-the-pocket expenses to any operator, it is of prime importance to [them] when making the decision to use a given fuel over another fuel."

Samuelson compared gasoline, propane, and butane under all engine operating conditions. He found fuel consumption was 18 percent higher for propane than gas at maximum load, but at anything less, it was

considerably better than gasoline. Butane performed similarly. LPG cost one-quarter what gasoline sold for, creating a substantial savings even with the greater consumption. M-M knew that others were looking at LPG. Ever the progressive company, M-M introduced a factory-built LGP-fuel Model U for 1941. Others considering the idea were derailed by the war. The government needed their factories for bombs and bombers, and the War Production Board limited fuel availability. Propane, like gasoline, was controlled, but because it was a by-product not used as tank, ship, or aircraft fuel, it was available. Still, until late 1951, M-M owned the factory-LPG market. Then Oliver introduced an LPG Model 77, and within another few years, every maker offered factory propane engine options.

The price of propane rose, yet diesel fuel remained comparatively steady. The additional consumption over gasoline became a liability as prices got closer and diesel efficiency became clear. M-M, first in, was last out, still offering Model G900 and G1000 tractors with LPG engines as late as 1970.

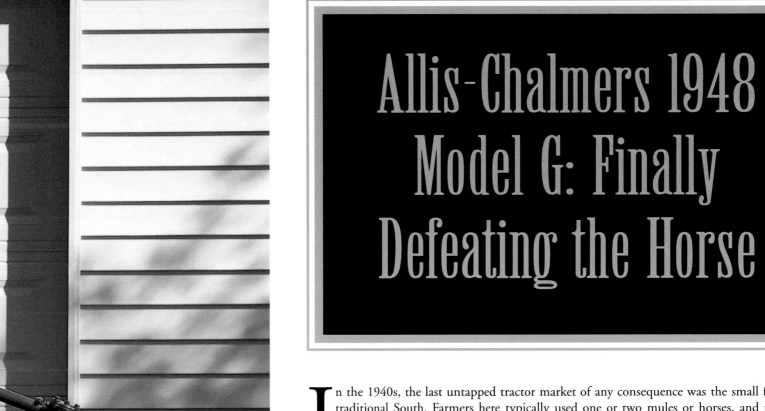

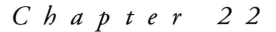

Allis-Chalmers 1948 Model G: Finally Defeating the Horse

In the 1940s, the last untapped tractor market of any consequence was the small farm in the traditional South. Farmers here typically used one or two mules or horses, and they firmly resisted mechanization for cost reasons as well as philosophical considerations. Allis-Chalmers' revolutionary Model B tractor and its imitators, especially Ford's 9N with Ferguson System and International Harvester's Model A, had taken care of the majority of small farms throughout the United States. Their influence, if not the actual tractors, had spread to Canada, the UK, and beyond. However the tobacco, vegetable, cotton, and other small growers of the South still couldn't—or wouldn't—be mechanized.

The temptation of all those potential sales was too great. Neither Allis-Chalmers nor IHC could ignore it. IHC introduced its Cub, a two-thirds–scale Farmall A, which it built in Louisville, Kentucky. Like IHC, Allis designed its own small tractor to take aim squarely at the horse. It would even be built in the South to minimize transportation costs. A-C selected Gadsden, Alabama, to manufacture its new Model G, as well as to produce a variety of electrical goods for other products.

The basic design concept of the G took inspiration from the experimental motor-cultivators produced in the late 1910s and early 1920s. Engineers stuck the engine and transmission at the rear to give operators an unobstructed view of the steering wheels up front and its cultivators below. They designed its rear engine/transmission pod to slip between crop rows. The braking system, devised to reduce width, earned Allis' design engineers one of several patents awarded to the Model G.

Yes, it was a garden tractor as well, but Allis-Chalmers meant it as a serious machine. The G was intended for the very last hold-out farmers using just one or two horses or mules on small spreads in the deep South. The company even chose to build the tractors in Gadsden, Alabama, to emphasize its purpose.

around St. Louis in April 1946. Wesley Park, apparently an Allis employee, worked with a local truck farmer testing which implements—mainly cultivators and planters—worked with the G's design configuration. Park encountered clearance problems with foot pedals and steering gear, not surprising considering the compact tractor's layout. Otherwise, the G performed well. Its Continental engine provided plenty of power. As Park described it, the tractor was planting straight and true. But the more that Park used it, the more he came to think some radical modifications might be beneficial.

Park's letter to a contact at the West Allis headquarters fairly bursts with enthusiasm and ideas:

I may get shot for saying this. But if this tractor was made about 12 inches longer in wheelbase, made to come down in tread, at least 36 or 34 inch tread, [and] make the front end heavier because it is light in front, although longer wheel base would help that part. Reason for the longer wheelbase is to have more room for implements and get it up farther in front for better vision, and also for mounting a trans-planter under[neath], which they are hollering out loud for. Then it should have a least six or eight inches more clearance overall. Now throw that torque tube away and make a double

The basic design concept of the G developed from motor-cultivators of the late 1910s and 1920s. Allis' engineers went a step forward, cantilevering the engine and transmission (in their own pod) off the rear axle, behind the operator to give the user an unobstructed view of the crop row and the G's front tires.

To support the front-end steering gear and front axle, engineers appropriated the torque tube they introduced on the Model B. Here, however, with no driveshaft to extend forward, the tube only connected the front to the rear as a kind of spacer.

The first prototype Gs may have appeared as early as 1943, but development resumed after World War II. However, one prototype underwent thorough testing

Looking smaller than it is, the G stretches out 114 inches, only 1 inch less than Ford's 9N. It also sits 4 inches taller, at 56. With its rear wheels tucked in as they are here, it's barely 36 inches wide. It weighs just 1,285 pounds yet could pull 1,096 pounds.

frame, twelve inches apart, and arch it from about six inches back of where the steering shaft part is now, over to the front axle, and put the steering wheel over to one side. Then you will have a perfect tractor for this kind of work.

The reason for just 12 inches wide with the frame is for 12 inch rows, then you can see all three. For wider rows [it] would not make any difference as long as you can see that center row. It is only natural and also force of habit, that you want to watch that center row, and it just can't be done in comfort by any means and for one row, that's awful, especially on ridges. I have helped that by setting the seat to one side, as I wrote before.

Parks also had discovered that firmly mounting planters to the round torque tube was a challenge that could be eliminated by using the parallel tube double frame. "Anything I might have to do here to help make it possible, I will do. If it isn't on the books, forget it, and say I did not write."

It must have been on the books. A-C made several of Park's changes. The G went into production and sold very well during its first few years. However, changes in the economy steered everything away from small farms and small tractors. This was, to some extent, a result of more efficient farming everywhere in the United States. Allis' revolutionary G met the company's

goal of mechanizing agriculture in one specific market for several specific crops. Allis discontinued the G in 1955. But the classic, simple design was far from dead.

Minneapolis-Moline produced a short-lived imitation. In the UK, David Brown manufactured a look-alike that remained in production for years. In the 1970s, a Wisconsin firm, GBT, built an imitation G using more modern components, as did the John Blue Co. of Huntsville, Alabama, with their G-1000. In the 1990s, Saukville Tractor, just outside Milwaukee in Saukville, Wisconsin, continued to produce tractors using the G's layout but with more modern engines and hydraulics. There may be other versions as well. Decades after Allis produced its last G, original models were still in strong demand from farmers as well as collectors.

Early prototypes used a continuous tube between the engine transmission pod and the front steering axles. Engineer Wesley Park informed the factory that the tube obstructed foot pedal and steering gear operation as well as the view of the row. he suggested the pair of arched tubes.

Model Gs used Continental Model N-62 inline four-cylinder engines of 2.375x3.5-inch bore and stroke. In its Nebraska tests in July 1948, the Continental peaked at 9.0 drawbar and 10.3 PTO horsepower at 1,798 rpm. Its three-speed transmission allowed it to top at 7 miles per hour.

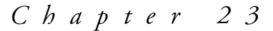

Oliver 1948 Model 88 Diesel Direct Injection Start

Even before Caterpillar engineers Art Rosen and Oscar Starr tamed lubrication problems with Diesel 65 Crawlers, the rest of the industry looked at this power source with great interest. Cat invested millions of dollars developing the engine. Then, in 1933, Cat had to spend hundreds of thousands more to solve the problems of cylinder wall scoring.

During this time, Cletrac introduced its big Diesel 80 crawler, using six-cylinder DHX engines from Hercules. Cletrac followed that in 1934 with what they called the Model 35D. The Model 35D became the 40 Diesel, using the Hercules DRX inline-six fitted with Bosch injection, a unit that provided a separate pump for each cylinder. Cletrac started its engines with a system devised by Leece-Neville, using "dieseline." Cat started its diesels with a two-cylinder gasoline "pony" engine.

In 1935, International Harvester brought out its McCormick-Deering WD-40 wheel tractor, with its own inline-six diesel. IHC started its engines by releasing a valve that created an auxiliary combustion chamber, fitted with a spark plug, which resulted in much lower compression. Operators started the engine on gasoline, and after a short warm-up, the system automatically shut the valves with a resounding pop and switched the engine operation over to diesel. IHC introduced a diesel crawler—TD-40 TracTracTor—at the same time, which started the same way.

Preheating the diesel's cylinders and turning the crankshaft against high compression were two great challenges. Allis-Chalmers began experimenting with diesels, as did Oliver Hart-Parr, each attempting to devise simpler starting techniques.

Diesel power fascinated the tractor manufacturers, but each recognized the problems with the fuel. In cold weather, it turned to jelly. Even in warm weather, with high engine compression needed to combust the fuel, starting was a challenge. At first it seemed starting directly on diesel was impossible. Oliver proved the industry hadn't tried hard enough.

Caterpillar's sales experience through 1934 and 1935 proved to its competitors that farmers were willing to spend extra money to buy a machine that gave them the greater economy and power that diesel engines offered. By 1935, the economy was recovering, and faith in technology and science—a luxury only a few years earlier when faith in everything was tested—was growing. The number of tractors on farms increased every year. American farmers added between 60,000 and 80,000 new machines per year during the mid-to-late 1920s, but this growth rate slipped to 16,000 for 1932 and only 13,000 for 1933. In 1934 the rate jumped back to 33,000 new tractors and to 52,000 in 1935. By then, there were 1,175,000 tractors on U.S. farms.

That year, however, diesel's magic dimmed with the introduction of Oliver's high-compression RC "70" model. This inline six-cylinder engine was engineered to burn gasoline with a tetraethyl lead additive that elevated the octane rating to 70 instead of 35 (kerosene), or 45 to 55 octane for earlier gasoline products. With simple electric starting, Oliver took almost every advantage back from diesel tractors—except the cost of fuel. It was incumbent now on diesel engine manufacturers to develop an easier starting system.

Crawler makers tried to reach the agriculture market with smaller diesels, such as Cletrac's ED in 1937

What it took to make direct starting on diesel fuel possible was a swirl-chamber combustion system fed by a single-plunger injection pump that used a "pencil" nozzle that directly shot vaporized fuel into the cylinders. Oliver's engineers and outside independents collaborated in the development.

Ironically, part of what made the direct-start diesel a reality was the tractor's sleek, slender styling by outside industrial designer Henry Wilbur Adams. He didn't leave enough room for the large multiport Bosch fuel-injection pump, so Oliver engineers improvised.

and Caterpillar's D-2 in 1938. Caterpillar had already introduced a full line, ranging from a three-cylinder Diesel 35 in 1933 up to the six-cylinder D-8 in late 1938. Allis-Chalmers brought out its HD-7, -10 and -14 models (the number indicating plow capability) using three-, four-, and six-cylinder two-cycle General Motors diesels. Still, these models started with gas and required elaborate switchover procedures.

As IHC introduced its first row-crop diesel, the MD, another fuel arrived in 1939: liquefied petroleum gases. LPG also required higher-compression engines. Just as diesel did, LPG yielded higher performance from a low-priced fuel. This initiated competition between the two. Unlike diesel but similar to gasoline, LPG-powered engines were easy to start.

In late 1940, World War II intruded on American industry. Experimentals went on a back burner as the federal government needed tractor, truck, and automakers to produce war materiel. As the war wound down, manufacturers recognized that pent-up demand for new machines would require new ideas that would have to happen just as soon as existing orders could be filled.

Experiments resumed in 1947, and Oliver readied its new Model 88 diesel. According to Herbert T. Morrell, Oliver's chief of engineering, the first 50 pilot-run diesel tractors used the swirl-chamber combustion system in the cylinder head (essentially a precombustion chamber designed by Englishman Harry Ricardo.) Oliver chose this system for its efficiency and also because outside industrial designer Wilbur Henry Adams had designed its new Fleetline tractors without adequate clearance for Bosch's large fuel-injection pump. Oliver design engineers Walt Roeming and Charles Van Overbeke replaced the swirl-chamber system with a single-plunger injector pump that fed all the cylinders, designed in 1947 by New York City power engineer Vernon Roosa. Roosa then devised "pencil" nozzles that directly injected fuel into the cylinders. Sundstrand Corporation quickly put the Roosa single-plunger injector pump into production.

This early version of Oliver's Hydra-Lectric hydraulic implement lift was operated by the two long levers below the steering column. Hydra-Lectric let farmers change an implement's working depth from the operator's platform while the tractor was in motion.

Oliver introduced its new Fleetline series of tractors to commemorate its centennial in 1948. The top of its line was the Model 88 three-to-four-plow row-crop tractor using Oliver's own inline six-cylinder engine. For production, Roeming and Van Osterbeke replaced the Ricardo cylinder head with one from Lanova, imported by Buda. (Oliver's 1930 diesel 80s were powered by Buda engines. The Lanova design used two teardrop-shaped tiny "Energy Cells" to improve fuel swirl.) This combination, along with their electric air intake heater, allowed the engine to start directly on diesel fuel. Operators no longer needed to resort to gasoline to preheat the engine, even when temperatures fell below freezing. To promote sales, Oliver offered a generous enticement: Buy their diesel and Oliver would refund half the cost of the first six months' fuel. Herbert Morrell reported that this cost Oliver—on average—just $44 per tractor. The promotion sold a lot of diesels and created widespread word-of-mouth enthusiasm. By 1954, Oliver boasted that more than 40 percent of all diesel agricultural tractors working in North America were Oliver-built.

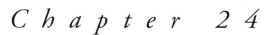

John Deere 1949 Model R Diesel

I t was Deere's most powerful tractor yet. It was the most trouble to develop, taking the longest to get right. But even before its dealer introduction in June 1949 in Manitoba, Deere knew they got it right. Months earlier, on April 19, Model R #1358 kicked off Nebraska University's 1949 testing season. In 57 hours of engine operation, a glass sediment bowl in the fuel line broke during the warm-up run. There were no other repairs or adjustments. Testers recorded its maximum drawbar horsepower at 43.15. Others had beaten that figure. Cat's first diesel cleared 65 horsepower, but it required 5.98 gallons per hour to operate. Deere's fuel economy, 2.8, was the best recorded, by far, of any tractor using any fuel.

Cat had perfected diesel power for tractor applications in the United States in 1931. Deere & Co., known for operating efficiency and economy in its "stove top fuel" tractors, couldn't ignore the diesel, no matter what difficulties might occur in development.

And there were challenges.

By late 1935, International Harvester introduced the WD-40, the nation's first wheeled diesel tractor. Deere's board of directors had already committed resources to develop diesels. While it competed vigorously with IHC, Deere's relationship with Caterpillar was friendly, largely from board member Frank Silloway's encouragement of Cat's unique products.

John Deere was not always first to innovate or even second to introduce. But before the company brought a product to market, it took time to get it right. When Deere brought out the product, it was the best. The Model R was Deere's biggest tractor up to that time.

In 1925 two California firms, C.L. Best Tractor Company and the Holt Manufacturing Company, consolidated their assets and products under the name Caterpillar. Since 1916, Holt had manufactured a side-hill harvester. Cat wanted to simplify its product line, and it offered the subsidiary, called Western Harvester, to Deere. Thinking Cat's price too high, Deere declined.

California's soil conditions gave birth to Cat's crawlers. But a lesser market existed among Caterpillar's customers for wheel-type tractors around the farm (and many Cat dealers recognized this). As Wayne Broehl wrote in *John Deere's Company*, Deere board member Frank Silloway (who steered them to the Waterloo Boy) proposed to his board a marketing agreement with Cat:

"We do not desire to manufacture track-type tractors," he said. "Through this Caterpillar [arrangement], we will have an opportunity to get into the industrial business in an important way." This opportunity did interest Deere.

Caterpillar was intrigued and responded to dealers concerned that Deere's two-cylinder engines did not follow the trends of other makers: Caterpillar itself had just introduced a two-cylinder diesel. Silloway hoped to lessen Deere's dependence on agricultural tractors and grab more of the growing industrial trade. He proposed sharing retailing, marketing, and, possibly, research efforts.

Whether Caterpillar's design engineers opened their facilities to Deere's experimenters is unknown. Jesse Lindeman, who devised Deere's Model BO-crawlers, had

The instrument panel hides the massive horizontal twin that Deere was most famous for. The R used a 5.75x8 giant of 416 cid. Thudding at 1,000 rpm, with an engine bark heard across a field, the R peaked at 48.6 PTO horsepower and 43.15 on the drawbar. In fifth gear for the road, the R would run 11.5 miles per hour.

The R was a big machine. Weighing 7,400 pounds, it stood 147 inches long, 78 inches tall, and 62.5 inches wide on standard 14x34 rear tires. (Fronts were 7.50x18s.) Over its five-year lifetime, Deere turned out 21,294 of these big diesels.

higher-voltage electric starting system—24 volts—but even that didn't heat the fuel enough or start the engine in the cold. Engineering tried different combustion chamber shapes to raise compression to 16:1 compared to 4:1 for kerosene engines. Early on, Miller wrote, engineers chose the open combustion chamber design over pre-combustion chamber configurations as more fuel efficient and easier to start. By mid-1940, Engineering had created the first MXs, prototypes that eventually became the Model R.

In April, John Deere kicked off the 1949 Nebraska test season with its Model R. It ran 57 hours, producing during its tests a maximum of 43.15 horsepower. Others had exceeded that, but no one beat Deere's economy of operation. The R sipped only 2.8 gallons of fuel per hour, better—by far—than any other tractor using any other fuel ever tested at Nebraska.

engineering friends at Cat who helped him through many details.

Deere's diesel development began shortly after the marketing agreements between the two were enacted. Deere's customers had begun demanding these engines. Yet, stories of diesel development hatched a frenzy of fictional reports of more cylinders coming, a prospect upsetting to some.

Deere wrote its dealers in late December 1936:

"We are again receiving reports, originating no doubt from competitive tractor salesmen, stating we were coming out with a four-cylinder tractor. This is propaganda, pure and simple, and there is nothing to this claim. WE ARE NOT MAKING A FOUR-CYLINDER TRACTOR, NOR ARE WE EVER THINKING OF MAKING ONE." (Capitals were theirs.)

Yet developing additional power through the diesel was not so simple. Fuel turned gelatinous in cold temperatures. Starting under such extreme conditions was difficult. A farmer could hand-crank until spring!

Merle Miller, in a recent history of the New Generation models, published by ASAE, reported that Engineering produced a series of horizontal two-cylinder diesel prototypes, known internally as the PX series, mounted in modified model Ds. They tried starting the engine on gasoline and running it until warm, when the farmer would switch fuel supplies over to diesel. By 1937 experiments led engineers to use a

Between 1941 and 1945, Deere ran eight MX prototypes on test farms in Texas, Arizona, and Minnesota. They built five more in 1945 and eight in 1947. By the time the Model R was released for production, the starting procedure was set. An electric starter cranked an opposed two-cylinder gasoline "pony" engine. Similar to Caterpillar's system, the pony warmed the diesel engine block and fuel. At a set temperature, the gas engine also propelled the starter, cranking the diesel main engine.

Henry Dreyfuss Associates got involved early. With massive cooling required for the two huge cylinders, the fan sucked field debris into the radiator grille mesh. Hinting at appearance that would become more familiar, Dreyfuss set the corrugations so they could be easily swept clear by a farmer wearing gloves.

Deere kept the Model R in production through 1954, manufacturing nearly 21,300. But for all its improvements, the two-cylinder engine had reached its limits. Farmers wanted more features. It could take two cylinders just to run power-steering and live hydraulic pumps. The demands for more power in the early 1950s were in conflict with the protests of branch office sales staffs in late 1936. In May 1953, chairman Charles Deere Wiman launched a development program for a new series, a new generation of Deere tractors. When the New Generation tractors arrived, their appearance was so striking and their performance so convincing that few people counted cylinders.

Chapter 25

Minneapolis-Moline 1951 Uni-Tractor

T he basic concept of the Uni-Harvestor was that a tractor and its implements should be integrated. Tractors up to that time used hitches or mounted equipment that was more of an afterthought than a preconceived notion. In many ways—and many instances— this was a carryover from horse-drawn implement days. The Uni power unit was intended to be a basic drive element for large mounted equipment such as combines, hay balers, and corn huskers. The resulting package was compact, closer to an agile self-propelled apparatus. It appeared (and functioned) as a unified whole, its elements logically linked with one another, rather than gathered together, paradelike, as a clumsy tractor appeared when hitched to a long combine or hay baler. The Minneapolis-Moline Uni could even be used as a regular tractor for tillage operations, although that probably did not happen often.

Although M-M's Martin Ronning gets credit for designing the Uni-Harvestor, its origin went back much further, through some of the most famous people and tractors in the business. The Ronning family was composed of individuals who would seemingly rather invent something and apply for a patent than read the morning paper; a check of patent listings suggests they made it a habit to do so almost as often as newspapers were published. Hundreds of patents were awarded to various family members over a period of several decades. These include such significant innovations as tractor cultivator patents that International Harvester had to license for its Farmall, and the "Rolo-matic" front end that Deere introduced for its row-crop letter series tractors.

The concept was that the tractor chassis might be useful—and adaptable—to a variety of farm functions, serving as the driving and steering element of implements mounted onto the chassis rather than pulled behind it.

The Uni-Balor was one of several mountable apparatuses meant for the Uni-Farmor system. Designed by Minneapolis-Moline's Martin Ronning, the idea of a power unit with interchangeable tools goes back to an Iowa inventor, John O'Donnell, in 1915.

Adolph and Andrean Ronning were Norwegian farmers living in Minnesota. They began the family's inventing tradition, and their children wasted little time before becoming involved. Among the many inventions that Adolph and Andrean patented was a system consisting of a power unit and a host of directly mounted tools. The power unit itself was invented (and patented) by John O'Donnell of Sheldon, Iowa, in 1916 (he applied for the patent in 1915). The Ronning brothers acquired O'Donnell's patent. It inspired them. Soon came other patents for cultivators, ensilage harvesters, binders, mowers and other tools, each of them meant to be directly mounted onto O'Donnell's creation. These patents came over a period of years. Still another patent covered a device to connect two tractors together, forming a four-wheel-drive machine. Each tractor had two main powered wheels, and two small auxiliary wheels were used for travel when the implement was not attached. Each implement had its own wheels and a rigid connection to the tractor power unit.

The Ronning brothers advertised these tractors, although it is questionable whether they manufactured any beyond a prototype or two. However, money still could be made in others ways. The Ronning family's patents stood directly in the way of IHC's new Farmall tractors by the mid-1920s. IHC ended up paying healthy licensing fees to the Ronnings for their tractor-mounted cultivator patents, and the ensilage harvester—a milestone in itself—was manufactured by IHC as a separate unit.

Nearly all of the patents were due to expire during the 1930s and 1940s. By then, self-propelled combines, produced by both Massey-Harris and International Harvester, already were sweeping the nation. A younger generation of Ronnings was ready. Exactly how Martin Ronning was related to Adolph and Andrean is unclear, but it seems certain there were blood ties. Creative

In April 1945, Martin Ronning sketched out the foundation of Minneapolis-Moline's Uni-Farmor system, a name presumably formed by combining the words farm *and* more. *Each implement mounted onto chassis frame rails that are capable of supporting more than their own weight.*

Ronning could not use a unitized-frame construction because he needed his machine to offer numerous mounting points for Uni-system tools. Its offset, high-front operator's position granted the farmer superior visibility steering through rows and put operators ahead and above the dust.

Early models used Minneapolis-Moline's 3.625x5-inch, 48-horsepower V-4 engine and steered with a single wheel. Revised in 1960, the Unis adopted the 5-Star 55-horsepower PTO-rated larger in-line fours and dual rear wheel steering to increase stability. Soon after, New Idea acquired the line from Minneapolis-Moline.

heredity certainly linked these men. From the time he was 15 years old, Martin had been developing farm equipment. He built a tractor in 1909 with a five-horsepower gas engine and a variety of binder and mower parts. He started working for others in 1927, first with Minneapolis Threshing Machine Company and then for Minneapolis-Moline.

In April 1945, Martin Ronning sketched out a power unit capable of handling a combine and a two-row corn picker. This was the foundation of the Minneapolis-Moline Uni-Farmor system the company introduced in 1951. The Uni-system grew to include not only the original power unit, combine, and corn picker, but also a picker sheller, a forage harvester, various headers, a hay baler, a windrower, and additional attachments from a variety of makers. A few other manufacturers imitated the system as well. M-M redesigned the power unit for 1960. It improved the operator platform, and encased the engine and mechanicals in stylish sheet metal. M-M also enhanced stability by replacing the rear single steering wheel with two.

In 1962, Minneapolis-Moline sold the system to New Idea in Pennsylvania. New Idea was a well-established manufacturer of implements including forage and hay harvesters, manure spreaders, and other tools. The Uni-system fit perfectly in their product lineup and under New Idea, it continued to sell well. The Uni-system was popular with dairy farmers who had a variety of tasks to perform, but most of them operated smaller farms without the budget for a fleet of specialized machines.

AGCO acquired New Idea in 1992, and under its ownership, New Idea phased the system out of production. The Uni-concept was passed over by ever larger farms. These larger farm operators had the means and the need for specialized equipment of increased capacity.

International Harvester 1954 Super M Torque Amplifier

Almost as soon as there was more than one speed for tractors, farmers and engineers wanted more than two. Even when there were four or five, the gear ratios never seemed to perfectly match the engine's peak performance to the best ground speed for the implement in use. By early April 1931, John Liggett, an engineer with John Deere Tractor Company at Waterloo, Iowa, had perfected a system that essentially provided half-gears. This was a method, as he described in his patent application, "to provide a gear reduction mechanism by means of which the tractor speeds are somewhat reduced to produce a corresponding increase in the drawbar pull of the tractor." The drawbar pull was directly related to amount of torque the engine produced. Increase torque: Increase drawbar pull. Torque is often defined as the pulling power, or the "grunt" energy of the engine.

Most tractor engines were already designed to provide as much torque as possible. When designing an engine, the surefire recipe for torque is a long-stroke crankshaft and small-bore pistons. Short of redesigning the engine, how can an engineer provide more torque? It's a simple matter of gearing. Liggett put it best:

"It has been found by experience that in certain hilly sections in the wheat country a tractor will stall by reason of the fact that it does not have enough power in low gear to be able to pull uphill certain types of heavy farm machinery, such as a combined harvester." Liggett proposed a gear reduction system placed between the engine crankshaft and the clutch, to let the engine continue at the best speed for maximum torque while allowing the tractor to slow en-ough to get up the hill or

International Harvester began experimenting with the idea of speeds in between gears in the mid-1930s, creating a system with four gears in two ranges for the TD-18 crawler. By 1943 engineers devised a variation using one lever but two clutches. Further development stalled until after World War II.

through the densest crops. Once the difficult patch was passed, the system could be disengaged, raising the ground speed again.

Liggett received his patent in May 1934, but Deere & Co. chose not to develop this idea further. The terms of the patent expired in 1948.

International Harvester engineers Ed Johnson, David Baker, and Cliff Rogers were also looking for ways to better match power output to speed. The solution they came up with was to increase the number of gear choices and offer an independent PTO. One year after Liggett filed his application for a gear reduction system, IHC applied for one on a six-speed forward-and-reverse transmission with independent PTO.

IHC engineers also devised a dual-range four-gear transmission for the TD-18 crawler. The operator moved one lever to select the gear while standing still, and another lever to change from one range to the other could be shifted while moving. In 1943, Rogers, William Bechman, and Joseph Ziskal applied to patent a variation on that using one lever but two clutches. The main clutch engaged the second clutch and the transmission to the

M-series Farmalls were International's powerhouses during the 1940s and early 1950s. Introduced in 1939 with 30.6 drawbar and 34.8 belt pulley horsepower, the Super M, introduced in 1954, raised drawbar output to 41.8 and pulley power to 46.3, nearly 40 percent increases while weight went up only 15 percent.

International Harvester had high-clearance tractors in its 1935 lineup, including Farmall F-30 HV models. Among the most fascinating models for modern-day collectors, the high-clearance models worked in Midwest row crops and West Coast bedded fruit and vegetable farms.

final drive. The second clutch engaged only a set of reduction gears within the clutch housing. World War II interrupted all further development work on it until just about the time that Liggett's patent expired.

In 1950, IHC assembled a prototype H-8 and M-8 tractor, each with the dual-range gearbox. Stretching other envelopes, IHC also enclosed a hydraulic pump within the rear-end case and developed an independent PTO from a shaft running within the driveshaft for this prototype. But field tests and feedback from operators must have convinced them that dual clutches were preferable to two gearshift levers. (In 1963, IHC returned to the dual-range system and the independent PTO when it introduced the 706 and 806 models.)

The result of all this work was the Torque Amplifier transmission, or TA. The system provided a planetary gear set (that was normally locked up) within the oversize clutch housing, providing a direct engine crankshaft drive to the transmission mounted just behind it. When operators reached a tougher area in the field and needed to maintain constant engine speed to keep power up yet reduce ground speed to get through the area, they disengaged the planetary clutch. This cut ground speed by one-third.

But just as IHC prepared to introduce the TA in 1951, it concluded that the system it used to keep the gears from "winding up" (engaging ever tighter against each other and therefore making shifting very difficult) was doing that on its own. Engineering substituted an overrunning clutch, a system with a built-in tension

relief, to replace the earlier band-type clutch mechanism for the planetary gears. This required reengineering the lubrication system and redesigning the TA mechanism and the clutch housing. This actually did increase effective torque by nearly half again. IHC finally got the new system into production in late 1953, introducing it only on the International Farmall Super MTA, and on the McCormick-Deering Super W-6TA models in both gas and diesel engine versions.

A year later, IHC brought out its Farmall letter series replacements and the TA came along as standard equipment on the International 350, 400, and 450 models as well as the W-400s, W-450s, and the gas International 600s. While the tractor was moving, operators pulled back a long lever mounted on the left side of the transmission case to use the TA (by disengaging the planetaries), effectively giving them a second range of five forwards speeds and a slower reverse.

IHC, however, was not done investigating planetary gears. Historian Guy Fay learned that IHC had patented a transmission that utilized three planetary gear sets. The combinations of gears engaged and disengaged gave the effect of many more speeds forward and reverse, and the planetary gears offered an additional benefit of being switchable while the tractor was in motion, a concept Ford developed several years later and called its Select-O-Speed.

The Torque Amplifier was a complicated system that actually used its own moving parts to increase the engine's torque. An overrunning clutch kept transmission gears from winding up, engaging too tightly. With rotating planetary gears, torque increased by nearly half over what the engine alone produced.

The gear-reduction system that somewhat reduced ground speed while keeping engine power—its torque—at its optimum level was the initial idea of multiple speed transmissions. Inevitably a speed "between" the gears was seen as ideal. Introduced with the Super M, International's Torque Amplifier was immediately successful.

Minneapolis-Moline 1962 G-706 Four-Wheel Drive

Dedicated four-wheel-drive tractors in the early 1960s were very expensive. They were built by short-line manufacturers including Steiger in Fargo, North Dakota; Wagner in Portland, Oregon; or the Canadian Versatile from Winnipeg, Manitoba. They were also built by such long-liners as International Harvester or Deere & Co. In fact, these tractors were too prohibitively expensive for all but the largest farm operators.

One company had been selling an affordable solution for some time. Elwood Engineering Company (Elenco) in Wisconsin had produced and marketed kits to convert normal two-wheel-drive tractors to a mechanical front-wheel-assist (MFWA) four-wheel drive. Farmers fit them on Ford, IHC, and other makes, doing the adaptations themselves or having local mechanics do the work. This drive system wasn't exactly a true four-wheel drive. It did very little to change the weight distribution other than adding its own weight in mechanical parts to the front end. Thus, owners couldn't add much power at the front without spinning the wheels. Elwood recognized this limitation; its kits contained running gear only, no engine modifications.

This idea had been around since the early 1900s when IHC's Ed Johnston had tried it on some experimental International 8-16s he created to evaluate four- and six-wheel-drive applications to small tractors. However, by the 1950s, the technology had matured to the point where a small company such as Elwood produced kits that could be attached to equipment produced by others. Many mechanical advances had begun in this manner.

The concept of four-wheel drive was one that predated the 1930 Massey-Harris General Purpose tractor. Yet by the time farmers and engineers reached the late 1950s and early 1960s, the idea had progressed to monstrous machines for enormous ranches. Minneapolis-Moline introduced an affordable four-wheel drive with this series.

Sheppard 1954 Model SD4-TC with Torque Converter

A torque converter in an automobile makes perfect sense. In conditions of heavy traffic, it simply makes stopping and starting almost as effortless as thought. Pressure on the gas pedal raised engine speed, which turned the converter's internal blades faster, increasing pressure on the driveshaft. But in a tractor where far heavier workloads are experienced for extended periods of time without stops and starts, would there be any practical advantage?

R. H. Sheppard believed so. In 1956 he introduced his SD-4 model with an optional torque converter. For Sheppard, this made perfect sense.

"Smooth starts, elimination of jerks, jolts and jumpy operation, and greater control" were advantages the company touted for its tractors. Certainly friction clutches and sliding gears worked under load seldom made for smoothness or subtle control. Wear and tear on couplings was brutal.

An electrical engineer working in the shipyards in Hamburg, Germany, is credited with inventing the fluid coupling. Around 1905, Hermann Foettinger realized that the huge diesel engine's power on a ship's propeller shaft could be applied with more control. He conceived a pair of facing, opposite-vaned disks, enclosed in oil, that had no solid connection between them. The engine drives an impeller forcing oil against the propeller shaft-side turbine, getting it to turn gently. After many experiments, Foettinger added a third set of vanes, which he named a "reactor," in the housing. This reactor, or stator, as it's now called, jams the oil back against the engine

It took wartime tank technology to prove the advantages of a torque-converter–type transmission to agricultural tractors. As tanks were essentially armor-shrouded crawlers, using similar technology, shifting on the fly was not possible. Tanks got hit as they stopped to shift gears.

For R. H. Sheppard, the torque converter made perfect sense, allowing smooth starting under heavy load at full engine power. The instrument panel advises operators to "stop engine to shift" from low range to high, meaning a complete halt with the engine running.

Because Sheppard conceived the torque converter as part of the SD-4 package, there is nothing except a small TC on the badge that points out this is something different. The cable extending through the dash changes range within the torque converter inside the transmission housing.

impeller, giving it more power and effectively increasing torque. Transmission engineers refer to this as torque multiplication (which is different from torque amplification) and they often quote effects as high as double the actual engine torque while using this three-vaned system. It was common to achieve torque 2.5 times what the engine produced.

Foettinger applied his invention to ships by the early 1900s. In England in the early 1920s, Alan Coats fitted several torque converters to small railroad engines built by Vickers of England. A prototype automobile appeared at the 1919 New York Automobile Show, but no one produced them for sale until 1930, when the English Daimler automobile offered them as an option; during this time Buick began experimenting with torque converters in Detroit.

Transmissions in automobiles, both in Europe and America, went through several incarnations and variations as each maker tried to find a smoother way to shift gears without too great a loss of engine power. Wartime applications improved the strength, durability, and adaptability of torque converters.

American-built tanks in the European theater became a target each time they changed gears. Like tractors, tanks needed to hesitate during shifts. Engine exhaust showed the enemy where the tank was. The Army approached General Motors to create a transmission that tank operators could shift on the fly. By late 1941, GM's Allison transmission division and Buick were jointly producing tank transmissions based on Buick's Hydra-Matic torque converter system that added a second torque-multiplying stator vane. The effect, while intricate in its oil flow characteristics, provided a great multiplication of torque, something like 6-to-1.

But none of this addressed the singular problem of farm tractors. Unlike automobiles with their jackrabbit starts and long periods of off-the-gas coasting, and different from the slow-speed maneuvering under light load to position a mounted cannon or a high-speed run

to escape attack that a tank encountered, farm tractors mostly work under nearly full load.

The fluid that is forced from impeller past the stator and into turbine blades absorbs most of the hard contact. Heavy work stresses occur on solid mechanical crankshafts, driveshafts, and axles when operators start a tractor with large plows in heavy soil or huge combines from a standstill in dense crop. This stress is all absorbed by the roiling fluid among those three whirling blades.

Farm tractors operate at maximum torque engine speeds, for hours on end, sometimes for days. Ground speed simply makes the job more or less efficient. Engine power is what's needed to get the tractor through the job without bogging down. To be able to match

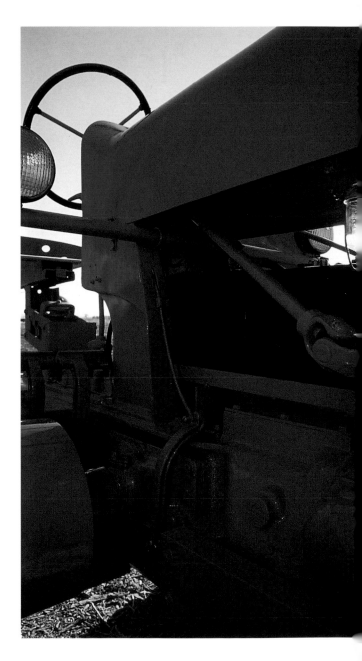

engine power to ground speed is what the torque converter could do best. Automobiles had three-, four-, or now five-speed automatic transmissions—tanks had four or six. Tractors, because of the variety of chores, needed six or more.

R. H. Sheppard, a Pennsylvania innovator who designed his own diesel engines and injection pumps, was the first to investigate torque converters for farm tractors. He produced a handful in 1955 and 1956, some say fewer than 50, others say no more than 10. These were the big four-plow-rated SD 4s with torque converters coupled to a 10-speed transmission. He conceived the SD-4 with the torque converter as an option so, other than a badge on the side of the tractor, nothing betrays what is different. His own tests showed his multiplication factor was 2.14-to-1, most effective at 1,540 rpm. He even directed the PTO output shaft through the torque converter, allowing implements to begin work more smoothly.

And then he stopped abruptly. Some said it was the cost of the unit, adding thousands to the already pricey Sheppard four-cylinder diesels. Others recall that the system was none too successful, leaving farmers with no power at all. Others wondered who needed it. Wasn't it just another gimmick for a market that had already rejected rubber tires and weather-shedding cabs? Now this?

The idea would reappear. International Harvester had proven the value of Torque Amplification.

The Torque-Multiplication of a converter made big engine power more useful. And shifting gears on the fly was not only valuable to tank commanders: Ford's product planners and engineers already had their own version in mind.

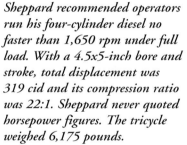

Sheppard recommended operators run his four-cylinder diesel no faster than 1,650 rpm under full load. With a 4.5x5-inch bore and stroke, total displacement was 319 cid and its compression ratio was 22:1. Sheppard never quoted horsepower figures. The tricycle weighed 6,175 pounds.

Other advice on the instrument panel tells operators to "warm engine 5 minutes at half throttle before moving." This was necessary to warm not only the diesel engine but also to heat up the torque-converter fluid to function properly.

Ford 1959 800-Series Tractor with Select-O-Speed Transmission

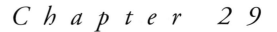

A s the 1930s and 1940s had been the "streamline age," so the 1950s became the Jet Age and the age of technology. For Harold Brock, chief engineer of Ford's Tractor and Implement Division, this meant much more than meeting the dictates of product planners. Brock also made certain that his engineers—not just automotive and truck engineers—got to have some fun, stretching technological envelopes.

In July 1957, Ford unveiled its "Typhoon," a free-piston gas turbine engine installed in a Model 961 tractor chassis. Engineering built three, each using 15:1 compression-ratio gas generators to produce exhaust gases. Expanding pressure forced hot exhaust through a turbine that drove a double-reduction gear to which engineers connected main and auxiliary drives. The auxiliary operated the hydraulic pump and PTO, while the main drive, reduced 5,600:1 in first gear, moved the tractor. The Typhoon's turbine idled at 10,000 rpm and under working conditions could see 43,000 rpm. Ford engineering limited output of the Typhoon to 50 horsepower, although 100 was available.

Ladysmith, Wisconsin, Ford tractor dealer Harold Ypma saw the Typhoon in late spring 1958 at the Minnesota State Fair. It made a lasting impression.

"A guy was driving it around. It had quite a sound. It howled pretty good. But even more than the sound was the Select-O-Speed. It had a gearshift wand. They never said a thing about that, just the guy was changing gears while it was moving by sliding that wand up and down. I was watching them shift the gears on the go. . . ."

This 1958 801 diesel ran on dual-rear tires to take full advantage of the power Ford's new Select-O-Speed transmitted from the diesel engine in this tractor. Unfortunately, early transmissions were plagued with troubles that ultimately forced a re-creation of the entire Select-O-Speed.

The idea was brilliant. It allowed the operator to select an engine running speed that provided the most power, whether connected by PTO to a harvester or doing simple tillage work. Then by moving the wand up or down, the operator could vary the ground speed to keep up with the workload.

This 1959 Model 811 industrial was fitted with an Elwood mechanical front-wheel-drive kit as a "Logger Special." This was a perfect adaptation for the Select-O-Speed in tugging felled timber out of forests, maintaining full torque no matter what the ground speed was.

coming down from 10th to 4th increased drawbar pull by eight times.

For PTO use over uneven terrain, the operator could shift down or up to maintain steady engine speed. This reduced the risk of any PTO-driven implement jamming. Top road speed was 18 miles per hour at 2,200 rpm in 10th gear; yet without changing engine speed, an operator could gear down continuously to 1.2 miles per hour in 1st gear.

Engineering a tractor is different from an automobile," Harold Brock said, "because the tractor is under more sustained load. On the transmission for an automobile, you can test it in low gear under full power and if it lasts forty-five minutes, it's a good transmission. In a tractor you put it in low gear and you have to run it thousands of hours. Because that's how tractors work.

In the reports that Ford published in SAE journals in July 1957, the transmission was briefly listed as a "full power shift, 10 speeds forward-2 reverse."

For the Ford Tractor and Implement Division, the introduction of the Select-O-Speed was as exciting as bringing into the world the Ford-Ferguson 9N with its three-point hitch and hydraulic system. Both challenged Ford's engineers thoroughly.

The first tractor assembled with the Select-O-Speed, serial number 60949, was manufactured on January 16, 1959. It was part of a fleet of Model 861 introduction tractors painted gold and provided to Ford's distributors. Not an automatic transmission, the Select-O-Speed was a system of four planetary gearsets in series, one behind the other. There was no longer a clutch, although an "inching" control allowed the tractor forward or backward movement with critical accuracy. The operator shifted gears hydraulically while moving, and Ford engineers conceived gear ratios that applied engine power efficiently. Downshifting from 6th to 4th gear doubled drawbar pulling power, while

There's a lot more of real engineering in the tractor. Today we do a lot of design and experimentation in computers before we ever build a prototype. With the 9N, most people working on it were not even engineering graduates. The master mechanics back then, technicians today, were engineering people doing the design work of those days.

We designed somewhat by proportion and somewhat by experience. We didn't have the sophisticated procedures and equipment we have today. We just over-designed things a great deal. We didn't know. So we always added more metal than we needed. Today you can nearly calculate how much metal you need. And because of the expertise, engineers sometimes make things too light. They get too close to the edge and they get in trouble.

The Select-O-Speed got in trouble. Early production models would not run very long before they'd fail, in some cases, just hours. The worst part for Brock was he and his engineers had no idea of a cure.

"It wasn't ready," tractor engineer Eddie Pinardi recalled, "it just wasn't ready." That frustrated the engineers. The only cure for "not ready" is more time. Brock had been under great pressure from higher management, product planners, to get the shift-on-the-go transmission out the door. The product planners wanted to be first.

"It wasn't one of those products," Pinardi explained, "where you could look at something, figure out what the problem was, fix it, and forever after it's a fine product. We could not find the problem. We brought in different engineers; they last a while and go back. The next set would come in and finally nobody wanted the job. Solve one problem and something else would go. We'd fix that. Then something else would fail. It wasn't as simple as gears overheating and failing." It was attributed to several causes, but in the end, the Tractor and Implement Division warranted a great number of tractors. "We finally redesigned the whole thing, based on everything we learned from all the fixes that didn't quite do the job. And then it went on to be a fine product. But by then, its reputation. . . ."

The Logger Special included a number of special pieces to protect the tractor and its operators. The heavy front bump bars and the stone (or stump) shield around the Elwood front differential were two distinctive differences. So was the elevated exhaust pipe, keeping exhaust heat high above sawdust.

Upper left: The 801 diesel used Ford's inline four-cylinder 3.9x3.6-inch engine with a 16.8:1 compression. Peak drawbar output at Nebraska tests was 36.8 horsepower while the engine produced 39.9 power take-off horsepower. This model, ready for its restoration, made use of a number of nonstock parts.

Wagner 1956 TR-14A Articulated Four-Wheel Drive

Frank Howard called the Wagner brothers "super-inventive." The Wagners each had their own interests, thinking up things for specialized needs that no one ever considered. Howard would know. He knew the Wagner brothers, and built tractors for them, years before he became service manager for Allied Systems, the successor to the Wagner Co.

By the late 1950s, the United States had 30 percent fewer farmers producing nearly three times the crops as in 1900. The baby boom had begun. Two new concepts, suburbs and interstate highways, consumed farmland outside cities. The labor force that had been paid to build tanks and ships on regular shifts with days off wouldn't return to farming's endless days. The trend began that led to larger farms. Corporations were not in it yet, but to survive the individual had to think like a smart business owner. When a cheap farmhand could operate a second tractor it made sense to have two tractors. Now with less help, larger holdings, and no way to stretch the seasons or slow the clock, every machine had to be more productive too.

Early four-wheel drive technology wasn't the great tool that users hoped. The Wagner boys, Eddie, Elmer, Ernie, Ervin, and Walter, built their first four-wheel-drive prototype in 1937. Elmer Wagner explained it in his 1958 presentation to the SAE.

"This required the solution of all problems which would permit a tractor to be rubber-tired, have four-wheel drive, four-wheel steering, free oscillation of both axles, high horsepower, high speeds, extreme mobility, sufficient traction and to perform farm work without creating any harmful compaction." That, Elmer knew, was a tall order.

The Wagners built their first four-wheel-drive prototype in 1937. While it was no great success, it taught them what they needed: high mobility and horsepower, sufficient traction along with four-wheel steering, and free movement of both axles. To accomplish this, they created the Pow-R-Flex coupling.

The Wagner brothers wisely decided to assemble the highest quality parts rather than spend the fortune to produce their own. They used a six-cylinder Cummins NH250 engine of 5.5x6 bore and stroke, 855 cid, developing 250 horsepower at 2,100 rpm. The Fuller 10-speed transmission provided an 18-mile-per-hour road speed.

Wagners of the 1950s and 1960s were crude compared to modern articulated four-wheel-drive giants from Deere and New Holland-Case-IH. This 1965 model boasted no sound insulation, compact disc player, cell phone, or global position satellite monitor to interfere with the operator's attention.

To do this, the Wagner Company created its "Pow-R-Flex coupling," the center hinge that connected the front and rear structural subassemblies of frame, axles, and wheels, called bogeys. Two steering pins (and one hydraulic cylinder) mounted to the front end, and oscillation tubes mounted to the rear, allowed the tractor to bend (or steer) and twist (or oscillate.) This flexibility, plus a transmission with internal chain drive to the front and rear driveshafts, provided full power to all four wheels at any angle of turn or twist.

Wagner was the first to offer an articulated four-wheel drive, their TR-9, to Nebraska for tests in September 1957. Steiger Brothers in Fargo, North Dakota, introduced their first models about then, but it was two years before they had regular production.

"Most of the world thought the tractor was too big," Frank Howard recalled. "But the guys in the big wheat country, Montana, Wyoming, liked it, they said, 'Because we don't have to listen to crawler tracks rattle all day.' "

One of Wagner's secrets of success (and some now say it's what hurt them) was that they built their tractors from the best elements of other people's catalogs. Engines came from Waukesha first, then Cummins, axles from Clark, transmissions from Fuller—always the strongest possible. Only their Pow-R-Flex was their own, meaning that if a part needed replacement, the owner could get it anywhere and not need to wait for Wagner to ship it. Wagner missed out on parts sales. But parts almost never needed replacement, and neither did their tractors.

John Deere liked Wagner's reputation. In late 1968, Deere approached Wagner president Jack Jacobs. Jacobs was sweating. The logging industry, a prime customer of Wagner log-kidders, was in recession. He was facing layoffs. Deere had no four-wheel-drive tractor. Deere let its big 8020 go out of production in 1966 and its replacement was far from ready. Competition was getting serious. Steiger had several models in production. Mississippi Road Supply, MRS, introduced models in 1963 and 1964. Versatile appeared in late 1966. Minneapolis-Moline, Oliver, Massey, and Allis each had

models in development. IHC already had powerful nonarticulated four-wheel drives in production.

Deere contracted to take all the Wagner Agriculture (WA) production of its two largest models, the 178-horsepower WA-14 and 220-horsepower WA-17, for 1969 and 1970, and open after that. The Wagner plant in Portland assembled the tractors in place, not on an assembly line; parts came to the tractor. Once completed, Wagner painted the tractors Deere green and yellow and affixed Deere decals. Production numbers for that period are sketchy, something like 47 of one model, 50 of the other. Deere constructed a warehouse in Portland to store them before sale. But the tractors didn't

really sell. In late 1970, Deere informed Wagner that its own Model 7020 was ready for introduction in late 1971. Deere only sold about 60 of the two models into 1971, and Frank Howard remembered that quite a few Wagners sat in Deere's warehouse for years.

Wagner's logging business and the demand for its compactor dozers had picked up, so losing Deere wasn't a crisis. But Deere's contract had a standard clause prohibiting Wagner from making competing products for five years. During that period, all major tractor makers introduced their own articulated four-wheel drives. By late 1974, most were restyling and redesigning second-generation models. For a smaller producer such as Wagner, it was all over. Well, not quite.

One very loyal, long-time Wagner customer in Montana begged Wagner to build him one more

WA-17. Because there was no assembly line, Wagner said, it was possible, but it would be costly. The rancher wasn't discouraged. It's absolutely the last, Wagner insisted, and the rancher agreed.

In late 1975, the first WA-17 in five years rolled out of the plant, painted Wagner yellow. Loaded on a truck, it headed toward Montana. Fifteen miles shy of its destination, there was an accident. The truck went off the road, and the trailer and tractor went over an embankment. The crash destroyed the tractor.

Wagner's insurance company made them return the tractor to Portland before they would pay. Frank Howard recalled that the tractor sat behind the plant for several years. Then, true to their promise, the Wagners went out and cut up the last Wagner agricultural tractor.

Wagners were meant for undulating terrain like north central Oregon, east of Mount Hood, where wheatfields roll on to the horizon. The big Cummins would pull 22,844 pounds in first, second, or third gears, more than enough for this John Deere 1610 39-foot chisel plow and Morris tine-tooth harrow. This WA-17 rides on eight 23.1-30-inch tires and stands 10 feet tall, 12 feet wide, and 20 feet long.

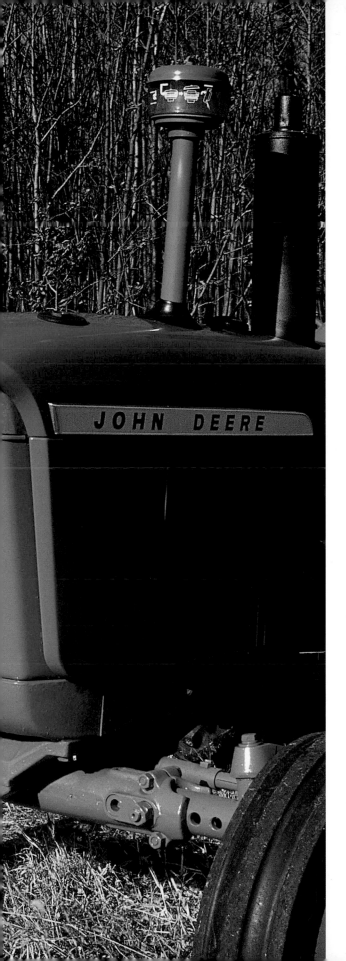

John Deere 1960 Model 4010 New Generation

"Every farmer is a born mechanic," the late Bill Hewitt observed. Hewitt was president and then chairman of Deere & Co., from May 1955 until his retirement in 1982. "And the two-cylinder tractor was the essence of simplicity. The good farmer could do a lot of the repairs on it. Even the absence of a self-starter made it easier." When Deere celebrated its 100th birthday in 1937, the tractor industry was manufacturing tractors averaging 35 horsepower. Then came Harry Ferguson's three-point hitch, and Harold Brock's hydraulic systems, power steering, and additional hydraulic systems to raise and lower front- and center-mounted implements. Tractors needed nearly 35 horsepower just to operate the hydraulics.

Before Hewitt became president, his predecessor (and father-in-law), Charles Deere Wiman, had authorized development of the two-cylinder replacements, to be called the New Generation. In April 1953 he ordered engineering to start fresh, carrying over nothing more than the yellow and green paint.

"Up until then," Hewitt recalled, "most of the improvements were 'improvements,' which modified the previous design. And the improved design came out and later it was improved. But each time it was modifications."

Wiman moved a task force out of day-to-day engineering at Waterloo and leased a small, empty grocery as they began considering what these new tractors had to do. The task force established a minimum of 50- and 70-PTO horsepower ratings for two models they coded the OY and OX,

Deere & Co. President Charles Deere Wiman authorized his engineers in April 1953 to begin work on tractors to replace the old reliable two-cylinders. Named the New Generation series, Wiman told the engineers they only needed to carry over green and yellow paint.

respectively. They created objectives for the new models including improvements in appearance (a better location for the LPG fuel tank so it did not project beyond the basic sheet metal), transmission (a PTO shaft access for the front of the tractor), and shifting (on the fly through a wider range of gears than the previous models). As Merle Miller reported in his recent book *Designing New Generation John Deere Tractors*, "the overriding performance objective was to give the farmer more tractor for the same or less money, and to ensure that it would do more work with less effort by the operator."

The engine development team first created a 45-degree-angle V-6 gasoline engine, then later a narrower 60-degree V-4 and V-6. Miller said that manufacturing costs and the excessive width of the V-type engines caused Deere to reject those designs. After several vertical inline efforts, they settled on designs with slightly longer stroke than bore to provide good torque, in four-cylinder versions for the OY (later the 3010) versions and sixes for the OX (4010) tractors. Deere selected the latest version of the Vernon Roosa–designed single-plunger injection pump, which Oliver had selected for its direct-start diesel engines. Unlike any previous diesel, Deere designed its engine without external oil lines that might become damaged or broken, possibly destroying the engine from lack of lubrication.

"The Waterloo people had already come up with a design and a kind of mock-up tractor when we got into this," Jim Conner explained. Conner was the man in charge of design for these New Generation tractors from Henry Dreyfuss & Associates. Their concerns were long standing: "Human Factors," or how to make any projects with which they were involved more operator-friendly. As Conner explained it, "Engineers are machine-oriented . . . , Dreyfuss' work is how the human interfaces with the machine." This meant more safety, comfort, efficiency, and convenience, improve-

The heart of the New Generation was its engine. The 4010 got a 302-ci vertical, inline six with 4x4-inch bore and stroke. Deere engineers struggled with how to mount the LPG tank, finally settling on vertical placement out front.

Once Waterloo engineers settled on an engine configuration, Jim Conner from Henry Dreyfuss & Associates began working on "human factors": how the operator platform fit and looked and worked. Dreyfuss' & Associates first began working with Deere in 1937.

ments his designers consistently sought from their first efforts with Deere in 1937.

"Our approach is not streamlining," Conner said. "It was to make a nice-looking tractor where everything had its reason for being."

Such philosophy seems extravagant without comparing the competition's offerings. Dreyfuss knew that most tractor purchases involved the whole family. If Deere's tractors were a mechanical match to IHC or Ford, but Deere's looked better in the field pulling plows or running down the road with a wagon, that might cinch the sale.

Dreyfuss cleaned up the operator's platform, relocating controls and instruments, and narrowed the cowl at the rear for greater visibility during cultivating. They introduced the "Human Factor Seat," created with Dr. Janet Travell, who gained fame as former President John Kennedy's back surgeon.

"Dr. Travell knew that as your stature increases, your legs get longer, your arms are longer, and you want to be further away," Conner recalled. "She figured out an angle, about 27 degrees, so our seat went up and

Deere hosted nearly 6,000 dealers and spouses to an introductory show, display, and barbecue in Dallas. When Bill Hewitt concluded the introductory program in the Coliseum, his guests had only seen these new machines from their seats. The multi-cylinder news surprised them. But when the faithful marched out the back door, they found $2 million worth of Deere's New Generation of Power that they could get close to: 136 tractors and 324 supplementary machines spread across 15 acres of the Cotton Bowl stadium parking lot.

For seven years, Deere had kept a secret. And after decades of company denials about building engines with more than two cylinders, and after a day-long introduction, Bill Hewitt recalled no one who complained.

This LPG-powered Row-Crop Utility 3010 was given the four-cylinder block, with identical 4.0x4.0-inch cylinder displacement. It developed 49.2 drawbar and 55.4 PTO horsepower at 2,200 rpm, while the LPG 4010 high-crop behind it produced 71.8 and 80.6 horsepower, respectively.

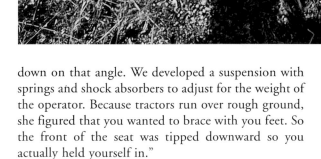

down on that angle. We developed a suspension with springs and shock absorbers to adjust for the weight of the operator. Because tractors run over rough ground, she figured that you wanted to brace with you feet. So the front of the seat was tipped downward so you actually held yourself in."

Prototype OX and OY tractors began field-testing in 1956. Deere hoped to introduce its New Generation in 1958. This included the development of transmissions providing eight speeds forward, and three-reverse shift-on-the-fly under full torque load, with a torque converter, known as a "power shift" transmission. Deere's vigorous testing of so many new systems led to problems, corrections, and improvements that held up introduction until mid-summer, 1960, D-Day, August 30.

Additional Dreyfuss input was the operator's seat, which moved away from the steering wheel and instrument panel as it rose up, allowing the taller farmer more room. Deere continued its practice of manufacturing limited numbers for small markets. This LPG high-crop was 1 of 17 built.

Allis-Chalmers 1961 Model D-19 Turbocharged Diesel

B y the 1960s, blown (forced induction) tractors were old hat. Allis-Chalmers had installed Detroit diesels in its crawler tractors starting in the late 1930s. These engines used Roots superchargers to help clean the cylinders of exhaust gases, crucial to Detroit's two-stroke design. Caterpillar had used engine-driven superchargers, and it was the first to introduce turbochargers, on its D-9 crawlers, beginning in 1956. While these Cats farmed in some areas of California and the Northwest, their use in construction and mining application was more common across the rest of the country. Although a few manufacturers overseas produced tractors with turbochargers (IHC was one of them, with a German tractor, the D-440, in the late 1950s), most American makers had resisted.

But the on-again-off-again horsepower wars resumed in the mid-1950s. Aftermarket suppliers offered add-on turbochargers for farm tractors, which appeared to be an easy way to upgrade power. One drawback was the tendency of these aftermarket kits to convert tractors into rolling shrapnel. The problem with these modifications was serious: engine and running gear were designed to accommodate specific power output and workloads. While engineers recognized the benefits of turbocharging, few manufacturers would accept the substantial costs to reengineer, design, and manufacture stronger components. Financial reality kept many of the wheel-tractor manufacturers away from turbochargers, until competition forced Allis-Chalmers' to consider them.

A photograph such as this often provokes the quip that this tractor was outstanding in its field. This is no joke with the impact of turbocharging on mechanized agriculture. Caterpillar introduced turbos in 1956 on its D-9 crawler, a machine meant primarily for agriculture, and Allis followed in 1961 with the industry's first wheel tractor.

its turbocharger so it's unknown what power that normally aspirated engine may have produced.) Soon, however, other manufacturers took the same step in order to fight the horsepower wars.

The first casualty of the horsepower competition were the tandem tractors. These appeared in the late 1940s as home-built creations to put more power under the farmer. Most commonly, these were two tractors joined together nose-to-hitch, and operated by complex linkages of controls. Manufacturers began producing their own connections that worked better but still required the expense of a second tractor. When IHC authorized its first U.S. turbo tractor, the 1206, in the early 1960s, its own tandem-tractor program died within three weeks, a victim of high manufacturing and retail costs and operating complexities. Once engineering strengthened crankshafts, main bearings, lubrication systems, and drivetrains, turbocharging represented a very cost-effective power gain.

Other casualties were coming. Allis replaced its D-19 with the One-Ninety series. Next, it built a higher-power version One-Ninety XT, which had a big 301-cid diesel with a larger turbocharger. This launched a grand tradition of Allis mechanics turning up the injection screw—way up. The power capabilities of this

The turbo (at the base of the large exhaust pipe just under the sheet metal) represented an extraordinary improvement once its great developmental challenges and costs were overcome. The D-19 went from 51.7 drawbar horsepower to 62.1 with the turbo, a 20 percent increase for a relatively small price increase.

Engineering had introduced to its sales department the new top-of-the-line tractor, a model designated the D-18. But this model had 60 horsepower, while the competition's top-of-the-line machines—Massey-Harris' 85, International's 660, and Case's 900—had a lot more. The D-18 went back to the drawing boards.

The engineers in West Allis thought they could get more power out of the gas and LPG versions with tuning, valving, and increasing compression. The diesel was more of a problem. So West Allis added a turbocharger and voila! More horsepower, although in truth, it was not much more. (Nebraska test results went up from 51.7-drawbar horsepower on the renumbered D-19 without the turbo to 62.1 with it.) Still, this was the first factory application of a turbocharger to a wheel-farm tractor in the United States, in 1961. (Caterpillar designed the D-9 for

With the introduction of the D-19 turbocharged tractor, Allis-Chalmers overnight killed another solution to the horsepower demand. Nearly every manufacturer had begun marketing tandem-tractor rigs, mating the front of one tractor to the rear of another. Very costly, and cumbersome to operate, the tandems quickly disappeared.

engine became legendary. Word spread. Everybody had to do it. Any mechanic could do it.

Then another word spread: powertrains began cracking. Mainly the torque tubes failed. Allis revised the One-Ninety XTs with strengthened drivetrains, and the frenzy began again. Since the drive train was stronger, mechanics could twist it tighter. New and used torque tubes became a premium item on the market, and they continue so today. If word spreads that someone once owned a One-Ninety, no matter how many years ago, phone calls tracked the owner down. Farmers, sounding slightly desperate, wondered if there were still good torque tubes lying around.

Turbos were not without their birthing pains. IHC experienced a curious problem. In development, they couldn't keep tires under their new 1206, essentially an 806 with a turbo. The horsepower transmitted through the tires literally ripped them off the tractor. Goodyear, Firestone, and other makers had to reformulate compounds and strengthen treads and sidewalls. Everyone benefited from these improved tires.

Power wasn't the only benefit of turbocharging. That was what everybody paid for. The surprise was the resulting, yet unexpected, change. Fuel efficiency improved measurably. Horsepower-per-pound of tractor went up; with Allis' D-19 diesel, it increased 7 percent. Noise decreased because turbochargers create a kind of muffling effect, although the whine from a turbo spinning at 80,000 rpm could be annoying, and some claimed it was injurious. Altitude effects were reduced greatly—no longer would most farmers on high plains and plateaus have to buy special high-altitude pistons. A turbocharger just jammed in more of the thin air.

Turbos are here to stay. At the present time, only base-level engines are naturally aspirated. The next level up is turbocharged. The next level above that has an intercooler. The intercooler reduces the temperature of the intake air, forcing into the engine a more dense fuel-air mixture, and putting out still more horsepower. And so it continues. Manufacturers experiment with multiple-turbos, smaller- and larger-diameter turbines, and air-to-air or air-to-water intercoolers. And they will continue so long as the horsepower race is on.

The D-19 begat the One-Ninety series, which introduced a new, larger engine with 301-cid. But it also brought with it a new technique, in which Allis mechanics turned up the injection screw, producing power at astonishing levels. There were, however, torque tube failures from the overload.

The perpetual horsepower race among manufacturers brought the turbo to A-C. Management set a target and engineers had two options: enlarge displacement of the D-18 from 262-ci to 290, or add a turbocharger. The turbo required stronger connecting rods, crankshafts, and bearings but did not require an entire new engine.

Chapter 33

John Deere 1966 Model 4020 Roll-Over Protection Systems

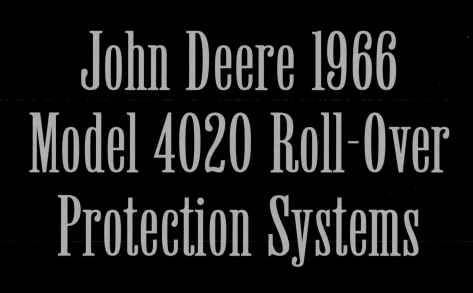

D. M. Hartsough's Little Bull tractor was a stubby tricycle driven by the larger of its two rear wheels. At $335, it sold like hotcakes: 3,800 copies in 1914. Probably America's first compact tractor, the Little Bull earned a more dubious distinction: Hartsough received the first patent for roll-over protection on May 4, 1915. Little Bulls tended to topple down hills when the drive wheel was on the downhill side.

Short, maneuverable, stable four-wheel tractors replaced Hartsough's configuration. One writer in 1919 observed, "Most tractors have enough power in low gear to raise the front wheels off the ground when the rear wheels are blocked." Fordsons suffered publicly for this trait, being the most widely sold, although even Best's and Holt's early crawlers raised their front wheel high in the air under load. Ford engineer Howard Simpson agonized over the risk to farmers. When Ford closed its plants in October 1920 during a short recession, Simpson spent three months developing rear fenders with long rear overhangs to limit how far the Fordson's nose came up. This was an option by 1923, but it provided no protection against tipping sideways. That problem remained for educators to solve—and many tried.

After World War II, University of Nebraska tractor test chief Lester Larsen, and Jack Steele, mounted a protective frame on a John Deere Model B and rolled it over 300 times in 10 years. They strapped stuffed coveralls to the operator's seat and filled a glass jug with water and catsup for its head. The tractor rolled, crushing the dummy and shattering the jug. The name "Jug Head" became

Tractor designers first became aware of the need for roll-over protection as early as 1914; tricycle tractors were particularly prone to tumble. Early efforts were aimed at saving the machine, and protecting the farmer's investment, not necessarily ensuring the farmer's safety.

Deere & Co. engineer Roy Harrington and product development manager Charles Morrison began developing a ROPS for the New Generation tractors in mid-1959. But the tractors were too close to introduction to accommodate the required modifications.

Merlin Hansen, Deere's chief engineer of new tractor design, and others knew if safety (which no farmer had asked for) was disguised as a sunshade (which many had requested), the customer might pay for it. Henry Dreyfuss & Associates chief William Purcell created the simple canopy atop the ROPS framework.

popular. At the universities at Montana, Massachusetts, and Cornell, faculty flipped tractors and smashed jugs to dramatize the danger to farmers.

Protection began appearing for crawlers when H. I. Blakey, a small manufacturer, patented a lightweight brush canopy in May 1948. Blakey's canopies saved a couple of operators when their crawlers gently slid over sideways in the Rockies. Word spread.

In late 1954 and early 1955, engineers at Sweden's National Testing Institute for Agricultural Machinery sent a test tractor fitted with a roll-over protection system (ROPS) down a steep mountain slope. While the ROPS survived, crashes destroyed expensive tractors, so the Institute developed laboratory tests swinging weights, pendulumlike, against the frameworks. The U.S. Forest Service conducted Tree-Drop, Tree-Fall, End-over-end-roll, and Side-Roll tests on crawlers with beefed-up Blakey canopies in November 1955 and June 1956. Their conclusions redirected thinking: "If an operator were to stay in the cab during the rollover—either front or side—he could guarantee his survivors that his body would not be crushed, but he might be dead." No one yet recognized what seat belts would do.

At UC Davis in 1953, Lloyd Lamouria met Ralph Parks, an Ag Extension engineer familiar with Larsen's Nebraska work. They fabricated a frame for a borrowed John Deere tractor. Ongoing efforts got expensive, but a benefactor appeared out of thin air.

Tom Soule, chief safety engineer with Industrial Indemnity Co. in San Francisco, had worked in mining. Soule and the others accepted that 40 years of patents and demonstrations had proven tractors dangerous. Every framework so far protected tractors but did nothing for the operator. Soule pushed roll-over protection, including "strong, form-fitting seats with safety belts" because "the driver is effectively guarded against injury no matter what happens to the tractor." Soule brought the Davis researchers $500.

Coby Lorenzen, an engineer and mathematician, arrived at Davis as Lamouria and Parks finished a new framework with seat belts. A Ford dealer loaned them a 740 tricycle and a Ferguson distributor provided them a Model 35 standard. Lorenzen attached stress-measurement instrumentation. Closed testing suggested minor design changes, but they were ready for the public, specifically a Pacific Coast region annual meeting of the ASAE in December 1956. The engineers printed 5,000 brochures and sets of drawings. Then a lawyer warned officials that the University might be sued if someone was injured while using this frame. UC cancelled the demonstration and pulled the printed material. The Ford dealer wanted nothing to do with the framework and no farmer would take it. They cut it up for scrap. Safety in the United States became something to be studied, but not necessarily implemented.

Sweden's reaction was very different. The government passed a law requiring new tractors delivered after June 30, 1959, to have an approved safety cab. In North Dakota, Warren Hansen, safety coordinator for the state highway department, fabricated and installed a high, wide frame on the rear axle of each highway mower tractor. Hansen's framework stopped the tractor from rolling beyond its side or tilting backward past the framework. His enthusiastic employees retrofitted all 190 mowers

before the 1960 season ended. Kansas and Illinois adopted similar mower frames.

At Michigan State University in 1960, Wesley Buchele and Alvin Bailey mounted a roll bar on a John Deere New Generation 4010 loaned by a local dealer. But a farmer told the branch manager he thought Deere's New Generation tractors "must be pretty flimsy—I see the University is already testing big roll bars to protect them." The researchers lost their tractor.

Deere's corporate attitude was very different from what universities were experiencing. Roy Harrington and Charles Morrison, manager of product development, fabricated Deere's first ROPS with seat belts on a New Generation prototype in mid-1959. Merlin Hansen, chief engineer of new tractor design, took personal interest in spring 1963, getting frames installed on every test tractor in Deere's fleet. His engineers concluded that safety measures were acceptable if they wouldn't obstruct fitting, or prevent using front or rear implements. Concerned that no farmer ever asked for protection, although many wanted a sunshade, Hansen made safety appealing. William F. Purcell, chief of design from Henry Dreyfuss & Associates, created a simple canopy atop the ROPS framework.

To make safety interchangeable, Hansen needed cooperation from full- and short-line manufacturers. He showed them Deere's confidential frame dimensions and test data. He knew farmers: If Deere alone had ROPS, farmers would buy elsewhere. Safety was an issue they didn't want to consider.

In March 1966, Deere led a meeting on ROPS with every major manufacturer, meanwhile preparing for June 14, when it announced its "Roll-Gard" and seat belts as an option on new tractors. Deere began delivering in October. Dealers displayed the tractors with ROPS at trade shows, farm expositions, and county and state fairs. They didn't sell. A Deere dealer in Tulare, California, drew a name from a hat for one of 3,000 ROPS that Deere gave away. The winner refused to take it home.

Sales efforts and steady urging from farmers' wives and families began ROPS' gradual acceptance. Incorporating ROPS into Sound-Gard cabs on Deere's 1972 Generation II models changed perceptions. Something sissified on Minneapolis-Moline's 1937 U-DLX, and stigmatized on Deere's 1966 4020s, had become civilized.

Deere introduced the "Roll Gard" ROPS in mid-1966 with a give-away program at state and county fairs. Safety was such an unwelcome subject that at least one winner, a farmer near Fresno, California, refused to take the framework home. Now Deere and others incorporate the technology into comfortable cabs.

Design engineers understood that ROPS might be acceptable so long as any framework did not interfere with mounting or operating any front or rear implements. But would the farmer pay extra for something like this? Deere chose to give away its research and design.

Chapter 34

International Harvester 1967 Model 656 Hydrostatic Transmission

Products aren't invented in a vacuum. Ideas are influenced by surrounding theories, unfilled needs, and nonrelated products. Great engineering merely advances ideas that had been temporary benchmarks in developments that came earlier. IHC's hydrostatic (Hydro) transmission is a perfect example.

P. M. Heldt, engineering editor of *Automotive Industries* magazine, reported in his 1942 book *Torque Converters* that hydraulic transmissions first appeared in the 1910s. But those inefficient, heavy systems consumed too much power to drive the pumps, leaving the crude engines little extra to push cars or trucks faster than a run.

By the mid-1920s in Europe, however, several firms produced railroad switch engines with hydraulic drives, and they performed well. In locomotives, weight was a benefit and their goal was never high speed. Hydrostatic drives also made reversing direction easy.

But because of size, weight, complexity, and the need for precise manufacturing, no one saw any cost benefit in trying hydraulic transmissions in tractors until 35 years later—especially when simply adding a third or fourth gear might achieve comparable results.

Competition always motivates engineering progress. Oliver Hart-Parr, and Rockol in Alberta, Canada, had joined Sheppard to offer fluid clutch models. Ford's Select-O-Speed moved Deere to introduce its Power Shift transmission. For International Harvester, the next step after its Torque Amplifier had to be fluid drive of some kind.

Hydraulic transmissions first appeared in the 1910s, but by the 1920s a number of locomotive switch-engine manufacturers used hydraulics. Reversing was easy, and weight was not an issue, but advantage and speed were never taken into consideration. But these elements limited other uses for an additional 35 years.

Competition among the manufacturers always resulted in engineering progress. After R. H. Sheppard introduced its torque-converter transmission, Oliver and others followed. Ford and Deere introduced Select-O-Speed and Power Shift transmissions, allowing shift on the fly. IHC followed its Torque Amplifier with fluid drive.

Meanwhile, in mid-1959, International Harvester completed an experimental gas turbine engine. Ford, Deere, Caterpillar, Boeing, Lockheed, and others tried to devise earth-bound applications for these aircraft engines. IHC tested these experimental engines and conventional engines with several transmissions.

Torque-converter inefficiency frustrated them. They continued to work at it, but they also looked elsewhere.

IHC engineers Carl Meile, S. S. Grossman, and D. F. Peck installed the gas turbine engine for another test in a prototype TD-50 crawler. They tested three power-trains: one was a gear-reduction into a torque converter; the second was a main hydromechanical transmission with a hydrostatic auxiliary drive to control steering; and the third used separate hydromechanical transmissions for each track with hydrostatic auxiliary drives for main power. A fourth model, built for comparison, used a 450-horsepower diesel through a torque converter. The three IHC engineers wanted to transfer huge amounts of torque to the ground without incurring catastrophic failures of drivelines such as had occurred with their large ag tractors. The hydros held up.

In mid-March 1960, IHC began to develop a full hydrostatic-drive research tractor based on its I-340 ag-tractor components.

Meile replaced the clutches, spline shafts, axles, and gears that propelled conventional tractors with full hydrostatic drive. A single hand control regulated continuously variable ground speed in either direction at constant engine speed. It also provided the functions of brakes using the same lever. Testers liked this feature; it allowed PTO-driven attachments true independence. For plowing, roto-tilling, or snow-blowing, they set engine speed for maximum torque, which

The 656 Hydro introduced continuously variable ground speed and braking functions without changing engine speed. It allowed operators to set the engine for maximum power while changing ground speed to accommodate dense crop growth or changes in terrain without compromising engine capability.

gave them full engine power from zero miles per hour up to maximum speed.

The first prototype used matching motors inside each rear wheel; the oil-plumbing configuration eliminated a differential. The prototype first ran in December 1959. Meile hoped to devise a power transfer system that, upon engaging forward drive under heavy implement load, did not exert extraordinary forces on drivetrain components. By mid-March 1960, he found an unexpected problem: under no-load at high speeds (road travel), pressure dropped in the pump. This affected hand control response; hydrostatic braking was non-existent. Meile added separate brakes, taken from the Truck Division.

IHC concluded that gas turbine technology was specialized and too costly. However, hydro transmissions encouraged them. In mid-1961, IHC developed a hydro option for the proposed 806 tractors. They split input power into a mechanical and a hydraulic power flow path. The mechanical path allowed a high level of efficiency, while the hydraulics made possible a stepless speed change. IHC (and other manufacturers) used the same oil for hydraulics, power steering and brakes, as well as for transmission and final drive lubrication. This new drive system took advantage of the common lubricant/transmission fluid. Development took time.

IHC always tried to apply its new technology. In mid-June 1962, it proposed replacing the existing gear transmission of the Cub Cadette. Other garden and lawn tractors used belt drives; IHC proposed a hydrostatic transaxle to eliminate clutches, transmissions, axles, differentials, and brakes, which reduced weight by 55 pounds. IHC completed a prototype a year later and tested it for months. The prototype convinced them a fully proven hydrostatic transaxle should be the first of an expanding family of hydraulic components.

IHC immediately planned for hydro transmissions for several agricultural and industrial models. Meanwhile, the Industrial Equipment Division installed torque-converter transmissions in certain models for shuttle-type operations, such as loading and dozing. Massey-Ferguson's Work Bull, and loaders from Rustler, Dynahoe, and Clark, already offered something similar.

IHC fitted its prototype hydromechanical transmission (designed in mid-1961 and painstakingly hand-built and bench tested) to a regular-production Farmall 806 early in 1965. A year of testing created an "exhaust gas ejector/heat exchanger," a kind of heat pump, to cool the transmission oil. IHC began production of an agricultural Farmall 656 and industrial International 2656 in October 1966 as 1967 models. But IHC wasn't done developing powertrains.

Some time later, engineers introduced a synchromesh transmission to replace previous sliding gear versions, especially for its largest tractors. A four-speed unit with constant mesh provided shift-on-the-go capability for unloaded conditions. It would not accomplish the full-load moving shifts that IHC's Torque Amplifier handled nor did it duplicate the variable speed characteristics of the hydrostatic. IHC offered it simply because it was the only maker providing synchromesh with an optional Torque Amplifier, advancing another temporary engineering benchmark.

Manufacturers had long shared hydraulic implement control fluids with power steering and brake systems. With the introduction of the Hydrostatic transmission, IHC found it could raise or lower the implement, steer front tires, and move the tractor forward or in reverse.

International Harvester 1978 Model 3588 2-Plus-2

T he Farm Equipment Research and Engineering Center (FEREC) was International Harvester's think tank. In the early 1970s it began experimenting with mating rear ends of two production tractors. While IHC bought large articulated four-wheel drives from Steiger, painted in IHC colors, it chose to develop its own mid-power range, designated the 2+2. This was a 1970s version of the tandem tractors offered in the late 1950s and 1960s.

FEREC engineers wrestled with where to put their cab. Did it go in the middle as Steiger, Versatile, and others did? IHC took advantage of a new final drive and set the cab over the rear axle. It designed its 2+2 series so that a solid front axle steered by pivoting the front half of the tractor, rather than turning the tires. Its long nose resulted from retaining the engine-before-drive-axle configuration of its two-wheel-drive tractors. This required no engine redesign and very little drivetrain modification yet increased the tractor's stability with heavy rear-mounted implements. IHC brought out the new 2+2 Model 3388 (130-PTO horsepower) and 3588 (150-horsepower) tractors in January 1979. A year later it brought out the 170-horsepower 3788 turbo diesel.

IHC watched Deere and Caterpillar introduce big technological jumps in the 1960s and early 1970s, machines that IHC recognized would be around for 10 years in order for the competitors to pay for them. The farm equipment market continued to improve. IHC chairman Brooks McCormick envisioned overtaking Deere in the 1980s as the industry's number one manufacturer. During the 1950s and 1970s, IHC had recycled 1940s and 1950s technology with disastrous and expensive results. Yet here was another example: its engine was new, powerful, and efficient, but its

This was essentially a late 1970s update of the 1950s idea of tandem tractors. IHC found this was the best solution to the need for mid-power-range four-wheel-drive tractors. IHC called them 2+2 because they were made of part of one two-wheel-drive tractor plus part of another.

IHC's engineers designed the 2+2 so it steered by pivoting a solid front axle and the entire front half of the tractor rather than just swiveling its tires. Hydraulics pushed one side forward and tugged the other back, similar to Wagner's Powr-Flex joint.

The long nose resulted from retaining the engine before drive axle configuration of IHC's two-wheel-drive tractors. Engineers knew that equal size front and rear tires improved traction, ride, and operator comfort. The 2+2 provided great stability and balance with heavy rear-mounted implements.

frame, drivetrain, and controls were simply updated pieces from the early 1960s. This practice would catch up with them.

Farmers bought equipment three times a year, prior to spring planting, before fall harvest, and in late December for tax planning. The cycle peaked every seven years; for example, 1966 was great and so was 1973. IHC anticipated 1980 but was pleased to find the cycle emerging in 1979, just as the 2+2s appeared.

Back in May 1977, IHC approved the development of new powertrains for several larger-horsepower tractors, along with a new pressure flow compensation hydraulic system. This combined project was called "MATH," Modular Axle, Transmissions, Hydraulics. It represented, in one tractor, the most advanced technology IHC could attempt: the final drive on two-wheel-drive tractors, and front and rear units on big 2+2s.

The greatest technical advancements were in transmissions, not surprising from a company that produced Torque Amplifiers and the Hydrostatic transmissions. Originally proposed in 1976, one concept included Synchro-Torque transmissions for introduction with 2+2 tractors. This advanced helical gear design required a "white room"—an extremely clean lab—to assemble internal parts. It incorporated a three-speed constant-mesh gearbox, a two-speed double clutch-pack Torque Amplifier unit, and a three-range constant-mesh set (3x2x3,) providing 18-forward and 6-reverse speeds.

Despite a general economic slowdown, Ford and Massey-Ferguson introduced new high-power two-wheel-drive tractors in 1980, and Deere began its new $400 million Waterloo tractor plant. J. I. Case had a new tractor line in 1981 as did Ford and Massey in 1982; Allis-Chalmers followed in 1983. If IHC were to remain in business, it had to continue the development of this new series of highly advanced tractors.

Yet the first 2+2s were troubled. IHC used too light a chassis. Its sophisticated Synchro-Torque transmission, was not ready as it used a sliding-gear transmission built with 1960's tooling that was worn out. The loose

tolerances were unable to handle heavy loads with such great traction. Tractors broke in the fields.

International Harvester was in serious trouble, headed toward record losses. In late 1980, IHC reevaluated the 2+2s. It produced 7,657, but sold only 3,790 in the United States and 534 in Canada. Revised 2+2's came out, but other problems confronted farmers. The U.S. government banned grain sales to Russia, providing European countries a windfall market. Then, President Ronald Reagan's fiscal policies greatly increased the value of the dollar, so few nations could afford American produce.

Yet, confident of an economic turnaround, New Holland, the old-line harvesting equipment maker in Pennsylvania, began looking for a tractor line. New Holland approached Case, which had suffered its own tractor losses in the early 1980s. Tenneco Inc. had owned Case since 1967 and its president, James Ketelson, was a former Case man. Ketelson faced two choices: abandon

ag tractors or get bigger. Case had quit the harvester business long before. The same surge that buoyed IHC's hopes in 1979 convinced Ketelson to sidestep New Holland and go after IHC's ailing Agricultural Equipment Group, with its innovative axial-flow harvesters.

Tenneco acquired IHC in late November 1984. This acquisition immediately reduced U.S. tractor production capacity by one-third, yet increased Case's market share to 35 percent, second only to Deere at 40 percent. Case produced about 20 well-regarded tractor models, including crab-steering four-wheel drives. New Holland asked Ketelson to sell IHC's 33 tractor models. Tenneco, fearing the competition, announced immediately that it would discontinue production of IHC's tractors.

Carroll "Kelly" Birkey, a dealer in Paxton, Illinois, for 35 years, was International's largest outlet for 2+2s. Birkey believes the millions IHC spent repairing early 2+2s helped kill the company. Engineering put out 24 field changes within the first two weeks.

"The 2+2s cost IHC dearly, as the company was struggling and did not have the resources to start from scratch, building the 2+2s on all-new components. Case had its own crab-steering four-wheel drives," he explained, "but the big articulated Steiger line came with IHC. Most dealers laughed at that long, drooping nose. They hated the 2+2 and refused to sell it."

Case and IHC engineers compared notes for future products; clearly IHC's new tractor line, with few changes, would stay. It was mostly Case tractors that died. But Tenneco saw the unpopular, costly 2+2 line and its antiquated Rock Island, Illinois, plant, and rejected both.

Despite IHC's problems, there were clear theoretical advantages to the design in ride and maneuverability. It's not inconceivable that this configuration will reappear in order to realize those benefits. "The concept was right," Birkey said recently. "What would have made the 2+2 work, made it acceptable? If Deere had taken it up and run with it, it would have floated. Deere is a smart company."

It took another company and another milestone to prove the wisdom of Birkey's words.

IHC introduced the 2+2 in both 250 and 130 power take-off horsepower versions in late 1978. But, sadly, the tractors had been manufactured at plants still using worn-out 1960s machine tools. Tolerances were loose and drivetrains couldn't take the huge loads that the 2+2's superior traction encouraged.

The 2+2s soon had two strikes against them. Mechanically, they couldn't take the abuse farmers were putting on them. Worse, dealers hated that long overhanging nose. In a world market buffeted by international politics, IHC was already stressed from construction equipment development costs.

1988 Caterpillar Challenger 65

I n mid-1983, a strange-looking D6 arrived at Paul Athorp's shops. Athorp was equipment manager for J. G. Boswell Company, a cotton grower in central California's San Joaquin Valley. Cat engineers had shifted the engine nearly 30 inches forward. They enclosed the operator in a cab. They replaced the front steel idler wheels with two rubber highway truck tires, and mounted hard rubber wheels on air-shocked trucks. A broad rubber belt with aggressive diagonal treads surrounded the exposed track running gear. They asked Athorp to work it hard. Engineers came to observe every week.

"We had a number of automobile wrecks that first year!" Wes McKeen recalled. He first saw the rubber-belted D6D in late 1982. He had assisted engineers testing High Drive steel-track crawlers. McKeen, agriculture tractor specialist with Tenco Tractor Company in Sacramento, helped place units on California farms. "People would be driving along, gazing at this strange-looking tractor off in a field or going down the road. We had people run into each other."

Caterpillar had tested a belted-track road grader clearing winter snows in Steamboat Springs, Colorado, during January 1981. A year later, Cat released the D6D and a D3B for agriculture tests. For a short time, it also ran a D4E, painted red and shrouded with unusual body panels to confuse observers. McKeen recalled that it worked.

"When we had the belted D3, we were driving it over on the edge of the freeway heading back to the store in Sacramento. A highway patrolman pulled us over. He got out of his car, looked at it, and said 'Oh, my gosh!'"

As early as 1981, Caterpillar began experimenting with rubber-belted equipment, a belted-track road grader doing snowplow duty in Colorado. The concept grew from customers who needed high traction, low soil compaction, and roadworthiness.

A series of six prototypes followed. The 855X-series more openly revealed the performance, shape, and sound of production versions. Engineers field-tested these "development mules" in central Illinois; Minot, North Dakota; Bluetown, Texas; Pullman, Washington; and Gila Bend, Arizona.

These machines often worked alongside competitors' double-tired articulated four-wheel-drive tractors at the same tasks. Early versions, 855X1, X2, and X3, tested first with parallel ribbed tracks; later efforts, X4, X5, and X6, used the production chevron pattern. The X4, X5, and X6 looked complete except for badges.

"It was like reinventing the wheel," McKeen continued. "The suspension was different, steering was different. That was the first time they came out with the direct-drive Power Shift. They went to a bogey air suspension on the mid-rollers. Caterpillar had developed and tested a four-wheel-drive tractor a couple years before. But they figured that was 'Me too,' and they had to do something different. It challenged them."

"Friction drive," Athorp explained. "Slam on the brakes on a steep enough hill and you don't have enough friction." Belts would slip on the drive wheels, so the engineers went through a process of increasing the belt tensions.

Powered by Cat's D-3309 638-cid inline six-cylinder diesel, with a bore and stroke of 4.75x6.0 inches, Challenger 65s made full use of their 271 horsepower engines at 2,100 rpm. A two-piece drive wheel inside the belt at the rear was connected directly to the output shaft of the final drive.

"The original Challenger 65s were at 10,000-pound belt tensions," he said. "They decided to go to 17,000-pound tensions. But Caterpillar doesn't just put a 17,000-pound tensioner in and let it go. This increased all the load on the entire structure. They pulled final drives out. Re-sized the bearings. I heard—no one would ever confirm it—the in-house costs to Caterpillar were $30,000 per tractor to upgrade."

For its efforts, Caterpillar received the 1987 "Concept of the Year Award" from the ASAE for Challenger's "Mobil-Trac™" system. The next generation, the Row-Crops, went out in the fields. Both Athorp and McKeen knew these experimentals.

Caterpillar had developed and tested a rubber-tired four-wheel-drive tractor before trying this system. While it was not without costly development challenges (hence, perhaps, its name), the Mobil-Trac™ system won for Caterpillar the 1987 Concept of the Year Award from the ASAE.

"We made our desires known," Paul Athorp said. "Farmers here want something like 5 1/2-pound ground pressure, and it appears that with this new Row-Crop Challenger we are probably somewhere between 6 and 9. We got around 25 to 28 with wheel tractors."

"Our goal is to be good cotton growers, not tractor developers or manufacturers. We were just like everybody else, modifying a piece of existing equipment to do our job better. We took what was brought out by the makers and worked to make it work for us.

"One of the things that happens with this new Challenger is interesting. The tractor is no longer the controlling factor. The factor that now controls how soon we can get into the fields is the implement behind it. We can go across ground with the Challenger, but the implement can't handle the wet conditions. It's a pretty dramatic change," Athorp said.

"The Challenger changed some things for us and for our competition," McKeen said. "We started selling Challengers to customers who had wheel tractors. Even here in California, customers who had articulated wheel-type high-horsepower tractors are using Challengers." He saw the future clearly: "This Row Cat may push John Deere and Case into building rubber tracks."

McKeen was correct. Case-IH announced its QuadTrac in 1996 and Deere & Co., followed with their 8000-series belted-track tractors in 1998. Caterpillar immediately filed a patent infringement suit against Deere. Deere won a summary judgment and dismissal on August 12, 1999; however Caterpillar appealed.

Those who've watched—and operated—both machines voice a marketing truth: When Challengers

first appeared in the Midwest, farmers viewed them as an oddity, only for growers in the West. However, when John Deeres arrived, it gave the concept credibility. Sales of Caterpillar Row-Crops (and standard Challengers) increased nationwide following Deere's introduction. An old axiom said it best: One is a fluke. Two is a trend.

This was Caterpillar's first steering wheel. Previously, crawler makers such as Cletrac had used steering wheels, which accomplished turns through a differential. Cat traditionally used steering brakes and track clutches, but with the belted track, it adopted differential steering from its ancestor, C. L. Best.

Track tension was a problem, and Cat increased it from 10,000 to 17,000, which required serious revisions. Low soil compaction is one of its strengths. The standard 30-inch-wide belts stretch 107 inches, spreading out its 36,200-pound weight at 5.6 pounds/square inch. Not bad for something 20 feet long, 12 feet tall, and nearly 10 feet wide.

153

Index